Nita Mehta's

101
CHICKEN
Recipes

Nita Mehta's

101 CHICKEN
Recipes

Nita Mehta
B.Sc. (Home Science)
M.Sc. (Food and Nutrition), Gold Medalist

SNAB
Excellence in Books

Snab Publishers Pvt Ltd

Corporate Office
3A/3, Asaf Ali Road, New Delhi 110 002
Phone: +91 11 2325 2948, 2325 0091
Telefax: +91 11 2325 0091
E-mail: nitamehta@nitamehta.com
Website: www.nitamehta.com

Editorial and Marketing office
E-159, Greater Kailash II, New Delhi 110 048

Food Styling and Photography by Snab
Typesetting by National Information Technology Academy
3A/3, Asaf Ali Road, New Delhi 110 002

Recipe Development & Testing:
Nita Mehta Foods - R & D Centre
3A/3, Asaf Ali Road, New Delhi - 110002
E-143, Amar Colony, Lajpat Nagar-IV, New Delhi - 110024

© Copyright SNAB PUBLISHERS PVT LTD 2003-2011
All rights reserved
ISBN 978-81-7869-066-7
3rd Print 2011

Printed in India by Aegean Offset Printers, Greater Noida

Distributed by :
NITA MEHTA BOOKS
3A/3, Asaf Ali Road, New Delhi - 02

Distribution Centre :
D16/1, Okhla Industrial Area, Phase-I,
New Delhi - 110020
Tel.: 26813199, 26813200
E-mail: nitamehta.mehta@gmail.com

NITA MEHTA
B O O K S
Distributors & Publishers

Price: Rs. 395/-

Introduction

'101 Chicken Recipes' offers your favourite meat cooked in many delicious ways. The chicken dish is the centre of attraction for any table spread and all the other dishes are planned around this main dish. Now you need not repeat the same chicken dish over and over again since you have a huge treasury of recipes.

Chicken is loved by people all over the world. There are different and imaginative ways in which chicken can be made. A successful chicken dish is one which is succulent, tender and cooked with the right amount of flavourings. This book offers various recipes each having its own distinguishing taste because of the right selection of spices in the marination and the method. Every recipe is explained with the minutest detail to give you delightful results. Wherever extra care and precutions are needed during the process, we have mentioned them very clearly, so that you just cannot go wrong. For example, if chicken is cooked on very high heat it tends to get hard as the protein in it toughens on high heat. Cooking on moderate heat is best for chicken.

Learn the cooking secrets and enjoy a variety of perfect chicken recipes.

Nita Mehta

CONTENTS

SNACKS   17

SOUPS AND SALADS 49

INDIAN 66

CONTINENTAL 99

CHINESE AND THAI 117

RICE, BREAD AND NOODLES 132

Buying & Storing Fresh Chicken

Chicken may be purchased fresh or frozen, whole or cut into pieces. The choice is for the individual to make, depending on how and when one wishes to cook it.

- Always buy broilers (young chicken of about 700 gm) when buying chicken as they are tender and cook faster.

- Do not buy a chicken with yellow skin and flesh. Buy one with white skin and flesh.

- Prefer picking fresh chicken to frozen. Fresh chicken is always more tender. If possible try and get it cut in front of your eyes.

- Chicken with bones is more tender than boneless chicken.

- When purchasing fresh chicken, make it the last purchase on your shopping trip. It is advisable to take along an insulated bag to place the chicken in to keep it cold on the trip home.

- Always buy skinless chicken. Get it cut into pieces as per your requirements. Ask the butcher to remove the excess fat from the chicken.

- When arriving home with your chicken purchase, remove from package, rinse and wipe dry with a paper towel. Cover loosely with plastic wrap. Extract air by pushing out towards the opening, & tape bag closed. Refrigerate immediately.

- Fresh chicken may be kept in the freezer compartment of the refrigerator for 3 days. If you want to store chicken, then buy ready frozen chicken than to buying fresh and freeze at home.

Buying & Storing Frozen Chicken

- When purchasing frozen chicken, check that the packages are not torn. Place in freezer immediately when you return home.

- Thaw frozen chicken thoroughly before cooking to avoid toughening the texture and to reduce the chance of some parts being undercooked. Undercooked parts could harbour food-spoiling bacteria.

- To thaw frozen chicken, remove chicken from freezer to the refrigerator, the night before or 6-8 before cooking It is always good to thaw the chicken in the refrigerator. Thawing on the kitchen slab on room temperature encourages the growth of bacteria and should be avoided.

- You can thaw chicken in a microwave also, if your microwave has a thawing mode.

- Do not refreeze thawed chicken. It is adivsable to cook the thawed chicken and freeze it when cooked, if you don't want to consume it immediately.

Sausages are meat mixtures, usually enclosed in casings. Salt, pepper, spices, herbs and garlic are often added to provide additional flavour and piquancy. As a rule, sausages tend to have a high fat content compared to fresh poultry.

Intially, sausages were prepared from pork, but now sausages are being prepared from chicken or lamb too.

Sausages are eaten whole as in case of hot dogs. Thick and big sausages are sliced to get slices as in case of pepperoni for pizzas, ham for sandwiches etc.

Salami, pepperoni, ham etc.. are all sliced sausages.

Buying Sausages:

- Sausages should look plump and well filled, without sagging skins, but not so full that they look fit to burst.

- They should look moist and fresh. Reject any with dried patches or ends, discoloured areas, or those that are wet, slimy or weeping.

- Smell is, of course, a good indicator of freshness and it is unwise to buy from a shop which smells unpleasant.

Storing Sausages:

- Leave pre-packed sausages in their sealed wrapper and store them in the coldest area of the refrigerator.

- Use before the expiry date given on the packet.

- Transfer loose sausages to a suitable dish and cover tightly with clear film (plastic wrap) or a lid, then use within two days of purchase.

- Be sure to keep highly aromatic sausages sealed under clear flim otherwise they are likely to taint delicate foods (particularly milk, butter) etc.

Techniques of Cutting Chicken

Different techniques of cutting chicken can only be done with boneless chicken.Only for tikka pieces you can choose pieces with bones. Your butcher will have to do it for you. Still I feel tikka pieces also taste best when they are boneless.

CHOPPING: TO CUT INTO SMALL PIECES:

Boneless chicken is cut into small pieces. Cut the chicken breast lengthwise into slices. Now cut the slices into small pieces which will result in finely chopped pieces.

SHREDDING: TO CUT INTO THIN, LONG PIECES:

Boneless chicken is cut into very thin, strips or shreds.

DICING: TO CUT INTO VERY SMALL PIECES:

Boneless chicken is cut into dice or small cubes. It is first cut lengthwise into ¼ or ½ inch thick strips/fingers and several such strips/fingers are kept together and further cut into ¼ inch pieces.

JULIENNES: TO CUT INTO THIN MATCH STICK LIKE PIECES:

The chicken is cut into very thin slices lengthwise.

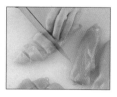

TIKKA PIECES:

Boneless chicken is cut into 1½" pieces.

How much should a chicken weigh?

Generally a tender chicken after cleaning weighs from 750-800 gms. It serves 4-5 people easily. Get it cut into 12 pieces.

Can chicken with bones be substituted with boneless chicken?

Yes. For ½ kg of chicken with bones use 400 gms of boneless chicken. Reduce the time of cooking for boneless chicken as it takes lesser time to cook as compared to chicken with bones.

How to cut chicken into pieces?

Chicken should be cut properly at the joints otherwise the meat tends to loosen from the bones on cooking.

Use plastic chopping boards instead of wooden boards for poultry. Why?

Wooden chopping boards can harbour bacteria. So go in for plastic ones or other non porous ones for cutting poultry. Still if you use a wooden board wash it well with hot soapy water after finished working.

Do not over cook chicken...

It tends to get hard. Use moderate to low heat for tender, juicy and uniformly cooked chicken.

Which utensil is best for sautening chicken?

For Indian style chicken use a kadhai as the masala doesn't stick to it. For sautening small pieces for Chinese and Italian use a frying pan.

Marination is important for grilling & tandoori recipes.

It helps to tenderize the meat and gives quicker cooking. It also adds a lot of flavour to the meat.

What is grilling/barbecueing?

This is cooking with direct heat. It is generally done in a electric oven or in a barbeque stand which uses hot coal to cook food. The food is placed on a wire rack. It is usually basted with its sauce or butter inbetween cooking to keep it moist. Tikkas are barbequed.

How to reheat an oven grilled chicken?

Bring your oven to 75°C/167°F. Place chicken and heat there for a few minutes.

My kebab/seekh mixture doesn't bind well and scatter on cooking. Why?

Grind mince once or twice in a mixer to give it a sticky consistency so that it binds well. Keep this finely churned mince mixture in the fridge for some time. Shape chilled mixture as required. Still if it breaks add 1 bread slice - churned in a mixer.

Home cooked chicken is not as tender as in a restaurant?

Stir-fry chicken over medium heat stirring constantly for the first 1-2 minutes. Very high heat toughens the protein in the chicken making it hard. Then cover & cook on low heat till done. Small pieces barely take 3-4 minutes to cook. Break a piece to check. If it tears easily and is no longer pink from inside, the chicken is done.

TIP...

Wherever the full breast is cooked, cover the breast with cling wrap and pound (hit) it with a rolling pin or a meat mallet. The breast gets thin and cooks faster.

Preheating oven...

The first thing when you start with the recipe is to switch on the oven at the temperature you want to bake. Preheat the oven for 10-15 minutes at the temperature stated in the recipe to get a well cooked dish.

I don't know how to thaw frozen chicken.

Frozen chicken should never be thawed at room temperature. So if the chicken is in the freezer, and you want to cook it the next morning, remove from freezer and put it in the upper shelf of the refrigerator (coldest part of the fridge), the night before.

How to boil and shred chicken for salads ?

Cut chicken into strips. Sprinkle chicken with salt, pepper and 1 tsp cornflour and mix well. Keep aside for 10 minutes. Boil 4-5 cups water. Add chicken strips and boil for 2 minutes till they turn whitish. Remove from water and use.

How to know if chicken is cooked from inside?

Break a small piece of chicken from the leg or thigh pieces. If it breaks off easily it is done. It should also not be pink from inside. It turns whitish when cooked.

14

Breast cooks more quickly than legs and thighs, so dont check from it.

When cooking poultry pieces, remember that breast cooks more quickly than legs and thighs. So if you want to know whether your chicken is cooked from inside or not always check leg or thigh portions. This will give you properly cooked poultry pieces.

How to place tikka pieces on a wire rack ?

Place the pieces with atleast 1″ gap between each piece so that each piece gets it's own space to cook. Cover tray beneath the wire rack with aluminium foil to collect drippings from tikkas.

Time limit of chicken ? ... shelf life

Frozen raw chicken can easily last upto a week whereas, cooked chicken should be consumed within 2 days.

TOMATO PUREE:

Tomatoes are roughly chopped & ground to a puree in a mixer. Instead of using raw tomatoes they are sometimes blanched. Blanching means to put the tomatoes in boiling hot water for 3-4 minutes and then plunging them in cold or tap water. This loosens the skin which is then removed. The peeled and slightly cooked tomatoes are then churned in the mixer to give a bright red puree. In contrast if the tomatoes are not blanched, the raw tomatoes give a pinkish puree and also the colour of the curry is then not so bright. These days ready made tomato puree is easily available.

puree of 3 tomatoes = 1 cup fresh puree

fresh puree  = *readymade puree*
(1 cup)   (½ cup)

Basic Recipes

These recipes are used in quite a few chicken recipes following later.

ONION PASTE:

Onions are ground to a paste in a mixer-grinder for many dishes.

3 onions = 1 cup onion paste (raw)

Tip:
When the onion paste is fried till light brown & is ready to add the masalas, sprinkle 2 tbsp water on the onions to prevent it from turning dark brown. Also remember to reduce the heat, as high heat will ruin the flavour of the masalas (spices).

Garnishes

Carrot & Radish Flowers: Take a slender carrot or radish. Peel and wash it. Make a sharp-angled cut, at about a height of 1½", about 1" downwards and inwards. Make 3 similar cuts from the remaining sides - all the cuts should meet at the end. Hold the top of the carrot with one hand, and the base with the other. Twist the lower portion to break off the top portion. You will have a tuberose in one hand and the remaining part of the carrot in the other. Trim the left-over carrot to get a pointed end. Make more flowers from the left over carrot. You can make such flowers with white radish also. Goes well with light French dressing salads.

Chilli Flower: Choose a slightly thick chilli. Cut into half starting from the tip almost till the end, leaving ½" from stem end. Cut each half with a scissor into many thin strips, keeping all intact at base. Put it in chilled water for 4-5 hours in the fridge. It opens up to a flower. Goes well with a spicy Thai salad!

Green Onion Flowers: Cut off about ¼ inch piece from the white bulb end and leaving 3" from the bulb, cut off the greens. Slice the bulb thinly lengthwise till the end of the bulb. Now make similar cuts at right angles. Similarly for a green side, cut the green leaves almost till the stem end to get thin strips. Place in iced water for some time until it opens up like a flower. A good garnish for a Chinese salad!

Tomato Rose: Take a very firm red tomato. Beginning at stem end, start cutting the skin as though you were peeling it in a long strip. The strip should be as long as possible, as thin as possible and about ½" to 1" wide. See that you keep changing the width of the strip as you go on peeling it. Do not let the strip be uniform in width. The rose looks more natural if the strip is cut uneven. If while peeling, it breaks, keep the broken part aside for use later on and continue cutting the peel. Now start rolling up the long strip firmly. Place it on the salad. Place the other parts of the strip around the rolled peel. The tomato strip should now look like a real rose. Looks good on a sour cream or mayonnaise dressing salad.

Snacks

Chilly Chicken Pizza

Makes 2

2 ready-made pizza bases, 150 gm pizza cheese - grated

TOMATO SPREAD

1-2 tbsp oil

4 flakes garlic - crushed and chopped finely

½ tsp red chilli paste or powder, ½ cup ready-made tomato puree

2 tbsp tomato sauce, 1 tsp oregano (dried), salt and pepper to taste

CHILLI CHICKEN TOPPING

1 boneless chicken breast (100-150 gm) - cut into ½" pieces

1 tsp red chilli paste (or *degi mirch*)

1 tsp soya sauce, 1 tsp vinegar, a pinch of ajinomoto (optional)

¼ tsp each - salt, pepper, 2 tbsp cornflour/plain flour, ½ onion - chopped

1 small capsicum - chopped, a few olives - sliced, optional

1. To prepare the tomato spread, heat oil on medium heat in a non stick pan. Add garlic. Stir and add tomato puree and sauce, salt and pepper. Add chilli paste or powder. Simmer for 2-3 minutes. Add oregano. Remove from heat.

2. For the chilli chicken topping, cut the chicken breast into ¼" pieces. In a bowl marinate with chilli paste or powder, soya sauce, vinegar, salt, pepper and ajinomoto for ½ hour or even more.

3. Heat oil in a kadhai. Drain the extra marinade from chicken pieces. Sprinkle flour and mix well to coat. Fry on medium heat till in 2 batches till light golden and cooked, 2-3 minutes for each batch. Remove from oil.

4. Add 1 tbsp of the prepared tomato spread to the chicken pieces to keep the chicken succulent and not turn too dry while grilling.

5. To assemble, oil the bottom of the pizza base with olive oil. Spread tomato spread on the top of pizza base, leaving the edges a little. Sprinkle most of the cheese on the tomato spread (reserve a little for the top). Spread chilli chicken, chopped capsicum, onions and olives. Sprinkle the remaining cheese.

6. Place the pizza on the wire rack of a hot oven at 200°C. Bake for about 7-8 minutes till the base gets crisp . Serve hot with chilli flakes and mustard sauce.

Chicken Parcels

Makes 10

10 pieces of aluminium foil - cut into 6" x 6" squares

FILLING

150-200 gm boneless chicken breast - cut into 2" long, thin strips

½ capsicum - shredded

½ carrot - shredded

2-3 flakes of garlic - crushed

¼ tsp crushed ginger

½ tsp each of salt, pepper, sugar, ajionomoto, or to taste

1 egg, 1 stock cube - crushed to a powder, optional

1 tbsp soy sauce, 1 tbsp sherry or gin or white wine

1 tbsp cornflour

1. Mix all the above ingredients of the filling together.

2. Place 4 chicken strips on a piece of foil. Arrange some capsicum and carrot on it. Roll upwards to get a long roll. Twist the sides lightly to seal the filling and give a toffee look. Refrigerate till serving time.

3. To serve, remove from fridge ½ hour before frying. Heat oil in a *kadhai* for deep frying. Put 3-4 parcels along with foil in oil. Fry on low-medium heat for about 4 minutes so that the chicken gets cooked. Serve hot wrapped in foil.

Chicken Croquettes

Makes 16

BOIL TOGETHER
600 gm chicken with bones
½ tsp salt, ½ tsp garlic - crushed, ¾ cup water

OTHER INGREDIENTS
2 tbsp butter, 2 tbsp oil, 6 tbsp plain flour (*maida*), ½ tsp crushed garlic
½ cup chopped mushrooms (4-5) or ½ cup chopped onions
½ cup milk, 1 tbsp finely chopped parsley
½ tsp salt, ½ tsp white pepper, ½ tsp red chilli flakes
2 cubes (40 gm) cheddar cheese - grated (4 tbsp)
1-2 tbsp finely chopped jalepenos or deseeded green chillies
2-3 tbsp corn kernels
1 bread slice - churned in a mixer to get fresh crumbs (½ cup)

COATING INGREDIENTS
1 egg white mixed with 1 tbsp water, 4 tbsp cornflour
2 tbsp finely chopped parsley
3 bread slices - churned in a mixer to get fresh crumbs, ½ tsp salt

1   Put chicken with garlic, salt and water in a pressure cooker. Keep on high heat till pressure develops or a whistle comes. Reduce heat and keep on low flame for 2 minutes. Remove from fire and let the pressure drop. Shred the chicken finely, discarding the bones. Keep the liquid stock aside.

2   Heat oil and butter in a pan. Add flour and stir on low heat for ½ minute. Add garlic and mushrooms or onions. Saute for 2 minutes.

3   Add boiled chicken and stir for 1 minute.

4   Add ½ cup stock and milk. Stir constantly till very thick and the mixture leaves the sides of the pan. Remove from fire. Add parsley, salt, white pepper, red chilli flakes, corn, jalepenos/green chillies, ½ cup fresh bread crumbs and cheese. Mix lightly. Check seasonings. Let it cool.

5   Shape into rolls. Roll on a flat surface to make uniform croquettes. Press the sides against the surface to get neat sides.

6   For coating, mix bread crumbs with salt and parsley. Roll a croquette over cornflour spread on a plate. Dust off excess. Dip in egg white. Again roll over cornflour and then dip in egg white. Finally roll in seasoned bread crumbs. Refrigerate till serving. To fry, heat oil on medium heat. Fry 2-3 at a time till golden. Drain on a paper towel. Serve with a dip or ketchup.

Stuffed Chicken Pinwheels

Makes 16 pieces

4 boneless chicken breasts (400-500 gm) - wash and pat dry

1ST MARINADE
1 tbsp lemon juice, ¾ tsp salt, ¾ tsp red chilli powder

2ND MARINADE
4 tbsp thick Amul cream (discard the liquid), 2 tbsp cornflour, 1 tbsp oil
2 tsp ginger-garlic paste, ½ tsp salt
1 tsp cumin (*jeera*) powder, ½ tsp pepper

FILLING
2 tbsp oil
2 onions - chopped finely, 1 tsp chopped garlic, 1 green chilli - finely chopped
¼ cup finely chopped mint/coriander
¼ cup corn, ½ green capsicum - chopped very finely
¼ tsp salt, ¼ tsp pepper, ¼ tsp red chilli flakes
½ cup grated cheddar cheese, ¼ cup grated mozzarella cheese
1 tsp lemon juice

1   Cut the breast from one edge almost till the other end, keeping it intact at the other end. Open up like a butterfly.

2   Rub chicken with lemon juice, salt and red chilli powder. Marinate for 15 minutes.

3   For the filling, cook onions in oil til golden brown. Add garlic. Stir. Add capsicum and green chillies. Stir for a few seconds. Add coriander/mint, corn, salt, pepper and red chilli flakes. Remove from heat and mix in both the cheeses. Add lemon juice to taste.

4   Mix all ingredients of the second marinade in a dish, big enough to fit the breast piece. Put the chicken in the 2nd marinade. Spread marinade on both sides of each piece.

5   Lay a chicken piece flat. Put ¼ of filling in the centre. Start rolling till almost the end. Pick up the other end and fold over to complete the roll. Marinate the rolls for 3-4 hours or overnight in the fridge. Keep them covered with a cling wrap.

6   To serve, cover the wire rack of the oven with aluminium foil. Grease the foil. Place rolls on it. Smear left over marinade on the rolls. Bake at 160°C for 25-30 minutes. If marinated overnight, baking time is only 15-20 minutes. Baste with oil in between. To serve, cut each roll into 4 slices with a sharp knife.

Teriyaki Chicken Skewers

Makes 15 skewers

300 gm chicken - cut into ¾" flat pieces

1 small green capsicum - cut into same size as chicken pieces

15 small mushrooms - cut stem in level with the cap

6-8 babycorns - cut into 1" pieces, optional

MARINADE

3 tbsp soya sauce

3 tbsp teriyaki sauce (ready-made)

1 tbsp lemon juice

¾ tbsp brown sugar

½ tsp ginger paste

1 tbsp garlic paste

2 tbsp oil

a pinch of salt and pepper

1. Mix all ingredients of the marinade in a low- sided dish. Marinate chicken, capsicum, baby corn and mushrooms in the marinade for 4-5 hours or overnight.

2. Skewer a piece of chicken, keeping it flat on the skewer. Thread a baby corn, then capsicum and a piece of chicken again on the skewer. Finally top with a mushroom, threading it sideways, so that it lies flat on the skewer. Keep skewers in the dish and cover with a plastic wrap. Keep refrigerated till serving time.

3. To serve, bring the chicken to room temperature by removing from the fridge about 30 minutes earlier.

4. Pan fry for 4-5 minutes in 2-3 tbsp oil in a pan (do not put too much oil in the pan) on medium heat, turning sides until cooked. Spoon the remaining marinade on the chicken skewers while pan frying to keep them moist and succulent. Serve hot.

Spring Rolls

Makes 8 rolls

PANCAKES

6 tbsp plain flour (*maida*), 10 tbsp cornflour, 1 whole egg, 1 egg white
¼ - ½ cup water, ½ tsp salt, or to taste, ¼ tsp white pepper

FILLING

1 tbsp oil, ½ tsp ginger - minced, ½ tsp garlic minced
1 egg, 1 onion - thinly sliced, 2 tbsp coriander - finely chopped
½ tsp salt, ¼ tsp ajinomoto, ¼ tsp pepper, ½ tsp soya sauce
150 gm thin strips of chicken - cut into 1" long pieces, 2 tbsp cornflour

COATING BATTER (CHILL BATTER)

3 tbsp cornflour, 3 tbsp plain flour (*maida*), 3 tbsp rice flour, 1 tsp oil
¼ tsp baking powder, ¼ tsp salt and pepper, ½ - ¾ cup ice cold water

1. In a deep bowl, mix plain flour, cornflour and egg. Beat well to the break all the lumps. Add salt, pepper and water. Leave aside for 15 minutes.

2. Heat a non-stick tawa or a frying pan. Smear it with oil. Wipe clean with tissue. Make sure that the pan is not too hot. Remove from fire. Put a ladle full of the batter in the centre of the pan. Quickly swirl it around to coat the surface of the pan evenly. Pour off the excess batter in the pan, back into the bowl to avoid making a thick pancake. Put the pan back on fire.

3. Cook till the pancake leaves the sides of the pan and is done, about ½ a minute, but not brown. Cook only on one side. Dust a flat work surface with cornflour and transfer the pancake onto it, cooked side up. Make remaining pancakes the same way, keeping 2 tbsp batter for later use. Stack pancakes one on top of the other ensuring that the previous one is dusted with cornflour.

4. Mix chicken, salt and cornflour. Boil 4 cups water and add the floured chicken to boiling water. Boil for 1 minute till they turn whitish. Remove from water.

5. Heat wok with 1 tbsp oil. Add ginger-garlic. Stir. Break an egg and scramble it for 5-10 seconds. Add onion and coriander and stir. Mix in the boiled chicken, salt, ajinomoto, pepper, soya sauce. Transfer filling to a plate. Cool.

6. Divide filling into 8 equal portions. Place one portion of the filling on the cooked side of a pancake. Moisten the edges with cornflour batter. Fold ½" from the left and right side, and then keeping the sides folded, roll upwards to get a roll. Repeat with other pancakes and keep in the chill tray for about 1 hr.

7. Mix all the ingredients of the coating batter. Chill the batter also. To serve, dip chilled rolls in cold batter and deep fry 1-2 pieces at a time on low medium heat and fry till golden. Cut into peices. Serve hot.

Club Sandwich

Serves 2-3

4 tbsp mayonnaise
200 gm chicken with bones
¼ cup finely shredded cabbage
¼ cup grated carrot
¼ tsp pepper
1 tbsp mustard sauce
1 cheese slice
1 small cucumber - wash & slice along with the peel into thin slices
1 egg omelette
6 slices white or brown bread
butter - enough to spread

1. Place chicken in a pressure cooker with ½ cup water, 1 tbsp oil, 1 tsp lemon juice and ¼ tsp salt. Mix well and pressure cook to 1- 2 whistles. Keep on low heat for 1-2 minutes. Remove from heat. When the pressure drops, drain chicken. Shred the chicken into small, long pieces. Discard bones. Keep shredded chicken aside.

2. Mix mayonnaise, ½ cup shredded chicken, cabbage, carrot, pepper and mustard sauce in a bowl. Mix well. Check seasonings.

3. Toast all the bread slices and spread some butter on one side of each bread. Place a cheese slice on a toast. Lay some cucumber slices on the cheese. Place another buttered toast on it, with the butter side down on the cucumber pieces.

4. Place omelette on bread. Spread some mayonnaise mixture on the last slice of bread and press on the omelette. Keep this sandwich aside.

5. Repeat with the other slices to make another sandwich.

6. Trim the edges of a sandwich and cut each sandwich diagonally into four pieces (use a sharp knife preferably with a saw edge for cutting sandwiches). Serve sandwich with french fries and tomato ketchup. To decorate the sandwich, pierce a small piece of lettuce or cabbage leaf through a tooth pick and top with a cherry. Serve.

Tip:
To save the sandwich from getting soggy : If the filling contains too much moisture, apply it just before serving or lay a lettuce leaf on the buttered bread before applying the filling.

Chicken Fingers

Serves 6-8

½ kg boneless chicken breast - cut into fingers
1 cup dry bread crumbs for coating
1 tsp oregano, 1 tsp red chilli flakes

MARINADE
1 tbsp ginger- garlic paste (1" piece of ginger & 8-10 flakes of garlic)
2 tbsp lemon juice, 1½ tsp salt, ½ tsp pepper powder
½ tsp red chilli powder, 4 tbsp cornflour, 2 eggs

1   Divide the chicken breast into two pieces horizontally (if thick) from the middle to make it thinner.

2   Cut the chicken into thin fingers. Pat dry the fingers.

3   Mix all ingredients of the marinade. Add the chicken fingers. Keep aside for 1-2 hours or even overnight.

4   Spread bread crumbs in a flat plate. Mix oregano and red chilli flakes. Mix well. Pick up one piece of marinated chicken and coat over dry bread crumbs. Coat and cover the chicken completely with bread crumbs on all the sides. Spread chicken fingers on a plate and cover with a plastic wrap. Keep in the fridge till serving time.

5   At serving time, heat oil in a pan. Reduce heat. Fry 8-10 chicken fingers on medium heat till golden and crisp. Do not fry on high heat otherwise the chicken will brown quickly without getting cooked. Let the chicken be in oil for 2-3 minutes to get cooked well. Drain on paper napkins to absorb excess oil. Serve hot.

Chicken Tostadas

Serves 6-7

3-4 tortillas (thin flour chappatis)

TOPPING

250 gm boneless chicken - cut into thin strips

3-4 whole dry red chillies (*Kashmiri* or regular dry chillies)

1 tsp finely chopped ginger, 1 tsp finely chopped garlic

3 spring onions - slice diagonally along with green part, (keep green part separately), ½ cup corn

1 tsp salt, ½ tsp sugar, 2 tbsp vinegar, ¼ cup grated cheddar cheese

½ cup yogurt - hang for 30 minutes, salt and white pepper to taste

a few jalapeno slices to top, optional

1. Soak whole red chillies in water for 15 minutes. Drain water. Grind chillies in a mixer to a fine paste. Use little water if needed for grinding. Alternately use ready made 1 tsp chilli garlic spread/paste.

2. Heat 5-6 tbsp oil. Add ginger and garlic. Fry for 1 minute.

3. Add chicken and fry for 2 minutes or till it changes colour.

4. Add 1 tsp red chilli paste, white part of spring onions, salt and sugar. Mix well.

5. Lower heat. Cover and cook for 4-5 minutes or till chicken is tender.

6. Add green part of spring onions, corn and vinegar. Mix. Remove from fire.

7. Cut out tortillas into small rounds of about 3" diameter.

8. Heat oil in a *kadhai*. Fry tostadas one at a time on both sides (1-2 minutes) till crisp. Remove and drain on a paper napkin.

9. Mix hung yogurt with salt and pepper to taste.

10. To assemble, top each tostada with hot chicken mixture, sprinkle cheese. Add a heaped tbsp of hung yogurt. Top with a slice of jalepeno. Serve immediately.

Chicken Shawarma Roll

Serves 2

250 gm boneless chicken - cut into thin long slices
2 pita breads - cut into two pieces horizontally to get 2 thin rounds
1 tomato, sliced and 1 onion, sliced - sprinkled with salt
Hummus, ready-made

MARINADE
1 tsp lemon juice or vinegar
½ tsp cinnamon (*dalchini*) powder
½ tsp ground cardamom
¼ cup thick yogurt (*dahi*), 1 tbsp oil, 1 tsp ginger garlic paste
½ of a well beaten egg, ¼ tsp garam masala
1 tsp salt, ½ tsp pepper, or to taste

1   Mix all the ingredients of marinade in a bowl. Add sliced chicken and keep aside for at least 4 hours or more in the fridge.

2   Heat 2 tbsp oil in a pan, add chicken along with the marinade. Stir fry for 4-5 minutes, till a little golden brown. Cook covered for 3-4 minutes or till tender.

3   Cut each pita bread horizontally into 2 pieces. Warm all the four pieces of pita bread on a hot *tawa* for 8-10 seconds. Keep one warmed piece on a flat surface. Spread 2 tbsp hummus, arrange chicken slices in the centre. Top with sliced tomatoes and onion. Roll forward to make a roll. Serve with hummus.

Chicken Wings

Serves 6

MARINATE TOGETHER
12 chicken wings (800 - 900 gm, choose small size)
1½ tbsp ginger-garlic paste, 1 tbsp soya sauce, 2 tsp vinegar
½ tsp pepper, 1 tsp salt, 1 tbsp oil
2 dry red chillies - soaked for 10 minutes in ¼ cup hot water

BATTER (MIX TOGETHER)
2 egg whites, 2 tbsp plain flour (*maida*), 2 tbsp cornflour, ¼ tsp salt
¼ tsp pepper, ¼ tsp ajinomoto, a pinch of orange red colour

COATING SAUCE
8 tbsp tomato ketchup, 1½ tsp vinegar
1½ tbsp soya sauce, a pinch of salt and pepper

1. Grind the soaked red chillies along with garlic and ginger to a paste. To this paste, add 2 tbsp soya sauce, 2 tsp vinegar, ½ tsp pepper, 1 tsp salt and 1 tbsp oil. Marinate the chicken wings in this paste. Keep aside in the refrigerator for at least 2- 3 hours or till serving time.

2. Mix all ingredients of the batter in a bowl. Heat oil in a kadhai. Dip wings in batter and fry 5-6 pieces at a time, keeping the chicken in oil for about 3-4 minutes in medium hot oil till chicken turns light golden and gets cooked. Keep aside.

3. To serve, heat 2 tbsp oil in a pan. Reduce heat. Add ketchup, vinegar, soya sauce, salt and pepper. Mix well. Add fried wings, stir for 2 minutes to coat all the pieces with the sauces. Serve hot wings immediately with chilli sauce.

Tip:
You can divide the wings into two pieces from the joint of the bone, if you want smaller wings. You can substitute other cuts of chicken for wings.

Kasoori Methi Kebab

Makes 10-12

250 gm chicken mince (*keema*)

1 onion - chopped, ½ tsp garlic paste, 1 tsp cumin (*jeera*) seeds

½ tsp garam masala, ½ tsp pepper, 1¼ tsp salt or to taste

5 tbsp dry fenugreek leaves (*kasoori methi*)

2 eggs - separate yolk and white

½ cup grated cheddar cheese

1 tbsp cornflour, 1 cup dry bread crumbs

POWDER TOGETHER

seeds of 3 black cardamoms (*moti elaichi*), 1" stick cinnamon (*dalchini*)

PASTE

5 flakes garlic, 1" piece of ginger, 2 green chillies

1   Wash mince in a strainer and press well to drain out the water.

2   Pressure cook chicken mince to give 2 whistles with 1 cup water. Keep on low flame for 2 minutes. Remove from fire. Drain, cool.

3   Churn in a mixer just for a second. Let it be rough. Do not churn more and make it too smooth.

4   Grind all the ingredients of the paste to a smooth paste.

5   Heat 3 tbsp oil, add cumin, wait for a minute.

6   Add onion, cook till soft.

7   Add garlic-ginger-chilli paste, cook for a minute.

8   Add crushed black cardamoms, cinnamon, garam masala, pepper, salt and 3 tbsp of dry fenugreek leaves.

9   Add boiled chicken mince. Mix well. Fry for 3-4 minutes.

10 Remove from fire. Add egg yolk, cheese and cornflour. Mix well.

11 Make balls, flatten it to give the shape of kebabs, 2" in diameter.

12 Beat egg white with remaining 2 tbsp of dry fenugreek leaves.

13 Dip kebabs in egg white mixture and then roll over dry bread crumbs.

14 Heat 4 tbsp oil in a pan. Shallow fry kebabs till golden brown. Serve hot.

Chicken Lollipops

Serves 3-4

600 gms chicken lollipops (ask the butcher to give you chicken lollipops or wings), oil for frying

MIX TOGETHER
1½ tsp ginger paste or 1¼" piece of ginger - crushed to a paste
1½ tsp garlic paste or 10-12 flakes of garlic - crushed to a paste
1½ tsp Kashmiri red chilli powder (degi mirch)
2 tsp dry mango powder (*amchoor*)
1 tsp garam masala, 1 tsp salt
¼ tsp tandoori red colour
4 tbsp plain flour (*maida*)

1. Mix together all ingredients written under mix together in a bowl.

2. Add the lollipops to the prepared mixture in the bowl. Let the chicken lollipops marinate in the mixture for atleast 3-4 hours in the refrigerator.

3. At the time of serving, give each piece with your hands a neat rounded shape.

4. Heat 5-6 tbsp oil in a pan, add 3-4 pieces at a time and shallow fry, turning sides or deep fry a few at a time till tender and crisp. If you shallow fry, keep the pan covered so that the chicken gets properly cooked while frying.

5. Drain on a paper napkin.

6. Serve on a bed of onion rings along with poodina chutney and lemon slices.

Chicken Tikka

Serves 6

500 gm boneless chicken - cut into 1½" pieces
some chaat masala and lemon juice to sprinkle

1st MARINADE
2 tbsp vinegar or lemon juice, 1½ tsp degi mirch, ½ tsp black pepper
½ tsp salt, 2 tsp ginger-garlic paste

2nd MARINADE
¾ cup yogurt (*dahi*) - hang in a muslin cloth for 1-2 hours
2 tbsp thick malai or cream, 2 tbsp cornflour, 2 tsp ginger-garlic paste
1 tbsp tandoori masala, 1 tbsp dry fenugreek leaves (*kasoori methi*)
¼ tsp black salt, ½ tsp chat masala, ½ tsp garam masala powder
½ tsp red chilli powder, 1 tsp salt, or to taste
2-3 drops of red colour, 2 tsp oil

BASTING
2 tbsp melted butter

1. Wash the chicken pieces. Cut chicken into 1½" pieces. Pat dry on a towel.

2. Marinate the pieces in the 1st marinade for ½ hour.

3. Transfer the hung yogurt to a flat bowl. Beat till smooth. Add all ingredients of 2nd marinade to yogurt. Beat well to get a smooth marinade.

4. Remove the chicken pieces from the 1st marinade. Add to 2nd marinade. Keep aside in the fridge for at least 3-4 hours or for overnight to allow it to absorb the flavourings of the marinade.

5. Heat an electric oven at 160°C or a gas tandoor on gas on moderate flame. Cover the wire rack or grill rack with aluminium foil. Grease foil with oil, so that the pieces do not stick to it after getting cooked. Place the well coated chicken pieces on it. If you like you can add some onions and capsicum to the second marinade and skewer the chicken and vegetables on bamboo or metal skewers.

6. Roast for 20 minutes till the coating turns a little dry. Baste with melted butter. Roast again for 5 minutes. If the tikkas are cooked and are still not brownish, you can put them under a grill for 2-3 minutes to acquire a tandoori look. Remove from oven. Sprinkle some chaat masala and lemon juice. Serve hot.

Tangri Bharwaan

Makes 4

4 chicken legs - choose legs which are broad in shape

1st MARINADE
1 tbsp lemon juice, ½ tsp salt, ½ tsp red chilli powder

2nd MARINADE
1 cup thick yogurt - hang for 60 minutes in a muslin cloth
¼ cup thick cream, 2 tbsp grated cheddar cheese
1 tsp black cumin (*shah jeera*) - roughly crushed, 1 tbsp cornflour
1 tsp red chilli powder, 1 tsp salt, a pinch of haldi, 1 tsp garam masala
1 tbsp ginger-garlic paste
1 tbsp barbecue masala or tandoori masala or ¾ tsp chaat masala
2 tbsp green coriander - chopped

FILLING
100 gms chicken mince (*keema*)
½ tsp cumin (*jeera*) seeds, 1 small onion - chopped
½ tsp ginger-garlic paste, 1 green chilli - chopped
1 tbsp chopped cashewnuts (*kaju*)
½ tsp salt, ½ tsp red chilli powder, ½ tsp roasted cumin (*jeera*) powder
2 tbsp grated cheese, 2 tbsp finely chopped coriander

1. Wash and pat dry chicken legs. Hit with a rolling pin gently to flatten it.

2. Marinate chicken with all ingredients of 1st marinade for ½ hour.

3. For filling, heat 2 tbsp oil in a kadhai, add cumin. Wait till golden. Add onion, stir till golden. Add ginger-garlic paste and chopped green chilli. Mix well.

4. Add chicken mince, bhuno on medium flame for 4-5 minutes.

5. Add chopped cashewnuts, salt, red chilli powder, roasted cumin powder and coriander. Remove from fire. Add cheese to the filling. Keep aside.

6. To make tangri, pick up a leg from the 1st marinade. Make a very deep cut, lengthwise on backside of leg with a knife. Go deep but see that bottom is intact, so that filling does not fall out from the other side.

7. With your fingers make maximum space inside the cut to stuff the filling.

8. Mix all the ingredients of the 2nd marinade together in a bowl.

9. Divide the filling into 5 portions. Make rough balls of each portion.

10 Fill deep cuts of the legs with one ball of the prepared filling. Keep stuffing the filling in the cut as much as it can take. Try and fill the maximum you can.

11 Holding each tangri carefully, spread the marinade all over, coating well on all the sides with the marinade. The legs should have a thick coating of the marinade. Let it marinate for atleast 2-3 hours or more.

12 Heat an oven to 180°C. Cover the wire rack loosely with a piece of aluminium foil. Grease the foil. Place stuffed tangris on it. Bake for 20 minutes. Baste (pour) 2 tbsp oil on the tangris & bake for another 15 minutes. Check with a knife, if chicken is cooked. Remove from oven. Serve hot with poodina chutney.

Potli Tikka Roll

Serves 6

2 chicken breasts (300 gm) - choose the ones that are wide in shape

1st MARINADE
1 tbsp lemon juice, ½ tsp salt, ½ tsp red chilli powder

2nd MARINADE
1 cup yogurt - hang for 60 minutes in a muslin cloth
4 tbsp thick cream, 3 tbsp dry bread crumbs, ½ tsp chaat masala
1 tsp cumin seeds (*jeera*), 1 tsp red chilli powder, 1 tsp salt
a pinch of turmeric (*haldi*) powder, 1 tsp garam masala
1 tbsp ginger-garlic paste, 3 tbsp dry fenugreek leaves (*kasoori methi*)

FILLING
5 tbsp black gram (*kale chhane*) - soak overnight or for 2-3 hours
1 tsp black cumin (*shah jeera*), 1 small onion - chopped
1 tsp ginger-garlic paste, ½ tsp chaat masala, ½ tsp salt
2 tbsp chopped coriander, 3 tbsp grated cheese (cubes)
drop of kewra essence

1   Make a slit in the chicken breast lengthwise (at the open side) almost till the end keeping the end intact. Open up to get a big heart shaped breast piece. Hit gently with a belan (rolling pin).

2   Marinate the chicken breast with the first marinade for ½ hour.

3   Pressure cook black gram with 1 cup water for 5 minutes on high flame. Strain, cool. Churn in a mixer to form crumbs.

4   Mix all the ingredients of the 2nd marinade.

5   Pick up the breast piece from the lemon juice marinade. Put them in the yogurt- cream marinade in the bowl. Spread marinade on both sides.

6   For filling, heat 2 tbsp oil, add black cumin. Wait for 30 seconds. Add onion. Cook till onion turn soft.

7   Add ginger-garlic paste, chaat masala and salt. Wait for half a minute.

8   Add black gram crumbs, bhuno for 5 minutes on high heat, stirring.

9   Remove from fire. Add coriander, cheese and essence.

10   To make kebab, take a marinated breast piece. Keep it on a flat surface. Spread ½ of filling on it, spreading all over completely. Press filling gently with the hand.

11 Start rolling forward from one side, to get a roll. When it gets difficult to roll, pick up the other unrolled remaining side and fold it over, on the rolled portion. Place the roll with the joint side down on a flat plate. Keep aside for atleast ½ hour in the fridge.

12 Heat an oven to 180°C. Place rolls carefully with the joint side down on the greased grill.

13 Pat remaining marinade on rolls nicely covering all sides. Roast for 20 minutes.

14 Pour some oil and roast for 10 minutes or till done.

15 Slice the roll into small pieces and serve.

Mila Jula Tikka

Serves 4

350 gms boneless chicken - cut into 1½" pieces (about 12 pieces)

MARINADE (MIX TOGETHER)

1 cup yogurt - hang in a muslin cloth for 1 hour

½ onion - very finely chopped, ½ capsicum - very finely chopped

½ tomato - remove pulp and chop very finely, 2 tbsp chopped coriander

1 tsp black cumin (*shah jeera*), ¼ tsp nutmeg (*jaiphal*) powder

¼ tsp mace (*javetri*) powder

½ tsp freshly ground black peppercorns (*saboot kali mirch*)

1 tbsp lemon juice or vinegar, 2 tbsp oil, 1½ tsp salt, ½ tsp chilli powder

½ tsp coriander (*dhania*) powder, ¾ tsp garam masala

GRIND TOGETHER

1 tbsp poppy seeds (*khus-khus*), ½" piece ginger, 5-6 flakes garlic

1 green chilli - roughly chopped, seeds of 3 black cardamoms (*moti elaichi*)

BASTING (POURING ON THE TIKKAS)

2 tbsp melted butter or oil

1. Wash chicken pieces. Pat dry on a kitchen towel.

2. Grind together poppy seeds, ginger, garlic, green chilli and seeds of black cardamoms with 2 tbsp water.

3. Mix all ingredients of marinade together in a bowl. Add khus paste. Add chicken pieces and let it marinate for 45 minutes or till serving time.

4. Heat an electric oven at 180°C or a gas tandoor on gas on moderate flame. Grease the wire or grill rack generously with oil. Place the well coated chicken pieces on the greased wire rack or skewer the chicken pieces. Pat the remaining marinade in the bowl on the chicken pieces.

5. Cook for 20 minutes, baste (pour) some butter or oil & keep again for 10 minutes. Remove and serve hot.

Italian Olive Bites

Serves 6

2 chicken breasts
15-20 green olives, preferably stuffed olives
3-4 tbsp finely grated cheddar cheese

MARINADE
2 tbsp olive oil
1-2 tbsp balsamic vinegar
1 tbsp crushed garlic
1 tsp mustard sauce, 1 tsp tomato ketchup
¼ tsp each of salt and pepper

1   Wash and pat dry chicken breasts. Chill in the freezer for 20 minutes. Cut chilled chicken lengthwise into thin, long strips. Chilling makes it easier to cut!

2   Mix all ingredients of the marinade in a bowl.

3   Marinate chicken strips in the marinade. Keep covered in the refrigerator for 1-2 hours or overnight in fridge.

4   Wrap chicken strip around the an olive and skewer through a tooth pick. Keep aside till serving time.

5   To serve, cover rack with foil and grease it. Place olive bites and sprinkle finely grated cheddar cheese on them. Bake at 160°C for 10-12 minutes. Serve.

Drums of Heaven

Serves 4-6

12 chicken wings - made into lollipops
2 tbsp soya sauce
1 tbsp ginger-garlic paste
½ tsp red chilli paste or red chilli powder
¼ tsp pepper
pinch of ajinomoto (optional)
¾ tsp salt, or to taste
oil for deep frying

BATTER (MIX TOGETHER)
1 egg, 2 tbsp plain flour (*maida*)
1 tbsp cornflour
¼ tsp of each - salt, pepper, ajinomoto and orange red colour

1   Marinate the chicken wings with soya sauce, ginger-garlic paste, chilli paste, pepper, ajinomoto and salt for 3-4 hours. Keep in the refrigerator.

2   At the time of serving, mix all ingredients of the batter.

3   Heat oil in a kadhai. Dip the chicken wings in the batter and fry in medium hot oil till golden and crisp. Serve hot wings with chilli sauce.

Chicken Dim Sums

Makes 14 pieces

STUFFING

200 gms chicken mince (*keema*), 2 tbsp very finely chopped onion
1 tbsp chopped parsley or coriander, ¼ cup finely chopped carrot
salt & pepper to taste, ½ tsp ajinomoto (optional)
1 tsp soya sauce, 2 tbsp oil

DOUGH

1 cup plain flour (*maida*), 1 tbsp oil, ¼ tsp salt

DIPPING SAUCE

5 tbsp soya sauce, 2 tbsp white vinegar, 1 tbsp oil (preferably olive oil)
4 flakes garlic - crushed to a paste
½ tsp chilli powder, 1 tsp tomato ketchup

1   Sift maida with salt. Add oil and knead with enough water to a stiff dough of rolling consistency, as that for puris. Keep in a cool place covered with a damp cloth for 30 minutes.

2   Put the mince in a strainer. Wash it in the strainer. Press to squeeze out the excess water. Add salt, pepper and oil and churn in a mixer grinder till the mince is very finely ground. Add onion, carrot and parsley. Keep stuffing aside.

3   Take out the dough and form small balls. Roll out flat, as thin as possible into small rounds of 2½" diameter.

4   Put some stuffing in the centre and make it into a ball. Roll the ball between the hands to give it an elongated shape like a roll.

5   To steam, put them in idlis stands or a steamer basket and steam for 10 minutes.

6   Let them cool slightly. Cut a slice from the top with a sharp knife to expose the filling. Dot with chilli sauce.

7   To prepare the dipping sauce, mix all ingredients in a bowl. Serve dim-sums with dipping sauce.

Crispy Baked Chicken

Serves 4

400 gms chicken drumsticks or lollipops

MARINADE

4 tbsp oil or melted butter

1½ tsp garlic paste or 12 flakes of garlic ground to a paste in a mixer

1½ tsp red chilli powder, 2 tsp cumin (*jeera*) seeds - powdered

2 tsp coriander (*dhania*) powder, 2" stick cinnamon (*dalchini*) - powdered

1 tbsp plain flour (*maida*), 1½ tsp salt

OTHER INGREDIENTS

2 eggs - beat well, ½ cup dry bread crumbs

1　Wash chicken well, pat dry on a clean kitchen towel. Prick with a fork all over.

2　Mix all the ingredients written under marinade in a flat bowl.

3　Add the chicken and let it marinate for 4-5 hours or overnight in the fridge. (The longer the marination time, the more flavourful your chicken).

4　Beat eggs lightly. Add ¼ tsp salt and ¼ tsp red chilli powder. Mix well.

5　Spread the bread crumbs in a flat plate.

6　Dip each chicken piece in egg and roll it in the bread crumbs.

7　Place on a baking dish and pour 1 tbsp oil or melted butter on the pieces.

8　Bake in a preheated oven at 200°C for 20 minutes. Overturn the pieces and sprinkle 1 tbsp of more oil or butter on the chicken and bake for another 20 minutes or till chicken gets properly cooked. Serve hot with ready-made salsa or tomato ketchup.

Chicken Kaathi Rolls

Serves 6

DOUGH FOR ROTIS
250 gm (2½ cups) plain flour (*maida*)
2 potatoes - boiled and grated, 2 tbsp oil, 1 tsp salt or to taste

FILLING
500 gm boneless chicken - cut into ½" pieces
1 large tomato - chopped, salt to taste, 1 tsp red chilli powder
½ tsp garam masala, 1 tsp lemon juice, 2 eggs - beaten
2 onions - thinly sliced & mixed with some hari pudina chutney

GRIND TO A PASTE
1 large onion, 1" piece of ginger and 8-10 flakes of garlic

1   For the dough, sift plain flour. Add grated potato, oil and salt. Mix well. Knead into a firm dough of rolling consistency with some water. Keep aside covered.

2   For the filling, heat 3 tbsp oil. Add the onion paste and cook till light brown. Add chopped tomato and cook till tomato turns soft. Add salt, garam masala, red chilli powder Add chicken. Cover and cook on low flame for about 8-10 minutes till chicken turns tender and dry. Remove from fire. Add lemon juice and keep aside.

3   Beat eggs and add a pinch of salt and pepper. Keep aside.

4   Make chappatis out of the prepared dough by cooking the rotis lightly on both sides on the tawa. Keep rotis in a casserole, to keep soft.

5   At serving time, heat tawa. Add 1 tsp of oil and fry the chappati on one side only. Do not turn. Pour 2 tbsp of beaten egg on the chappati and flip (turn) the roti to cook the egg. Remove from tawa, keeping the egg coated side up.

6   Sprinkle 1 tsp lemon juice on the egg coated side of the roti. Arrange chicken filling on one end of the roti. Sprinkle some onions on the filling and roll the roti forward tightly to form the Kaathi Roti. Serve hot.

Tandoori Chicken

Serves 4-5

1 small sized chicken (800 gm) - cut into 8 pieces

1 onion - grated, 4 tbsp oil

1 cup yogurt - hang in a muslin cloth for 1 hour

2 tbsp plain flour (*maida*)

3 tsp ginger-garlic paste

a pinch of orange red colour

2 tbsp dry fenugreek leaves (*kasoori methi*)

½ tsp cumin (*jeera*) powder

½ tsp coriander (*dhania*) powder

½ tsp garam masala powder

½ tbsp tandoori masala

1 tsp dry mango powder (amchoor)

1½ tsp salt

1 tsp degi mirch powder

1. Heat 4 tbsp oil and cook grated onion in it till golden brown. Remove from fire. Let it cool.

2. Mix hung yogurt, plain flour, colour and all other ingredients. Add enough colour to get a bright orange colour. Add the onion paste cooked in oil along with the remaining oil.

3. Wash chicken. Squeeze out all excess water. Pat dry on a clean kitchen towel.

4. Marinate chicken in the yogurt mixture for 2-3 hours in the refrigerator.

5. Rub the wire rack of the oven with oil and place the marinated chicken on it, so that the extra marinade can drip down from the grill. If the chicken is placed in a dish or a tray, the extra marinade and liquid keep collecting around the chicken pieces and hence they do not turn dry and crisp.

6. Roast for 8-10 minutes in an oven at 180°C. Overturn again, baste (pour) with 2 tbsp oil and cook for another 10-12 minutes or till tender and crisp.

7. Serve hot garnished with onion rings.

Tip:

- Instead of a full chicken only drumsticks (legs) can be made. They are called tangdi kebabs. After grilling, wrap a piece of aluminium foil at the end of each leg. Besides looking nice, it is also convenient for holding and eating the chicken leg.
- Boneless chicken cut into 1½"-2" pieces can be cooked in a similar manner to get chicken tikka.
- The grilled chicken can be added to an onion-tomato masala for a tikka masala dish.

Chilli Chicken

Serves 4

300 gm boneless chicken - cut into ½" cubes, 1 egg
2 tbsp cornflour, 2 tbsp plain flour (*maida*)
¾ tsp salt, ¼ tsp pepper, 1 tbsp garlic - crushed
1 tsp soya sauce, 1 tsp red chilli paste or red chilli sauce

OTHER INGREDIENTS
½ green, ½ yellow and ½ red capsicum - cut into 1" pieces, 3 tbsp oil
1 tbsp garlic - chopped very finely, 2 fresh green chillies - cut into 1" pieces
½ onion - cut into 4 pieces and separated, ½ tsp salt, ½ tsp pepper
a pinch of ajinomoto, a pinch sugar, or to taste, 1 tbsp soya sauce
1 tsp vinegar, or to taste, 4 tbsp tomato ketchup, 3 tbsp red chilli sauce
1 tbsp cornflour - dissolved in ½ cup water

1   Wash and pat dry chicken.

2   Mix cornflour and plain flour in a bowl. Add egg and mix very well to break all lumps. Add 1 tsp soya sauce, 1 tsp red chilli paste, salt, pepper and garlic. Add chicken to this mixture and keep aside for 20 minutes.

3   Heat oil for deep frying in a kadhai. Reduce heat. Add all chicken pieces and then increase heat. Fry for 2-3 minutes only till they turn very light golden. Do not fry longer as it will turn the chicken hard. Keep aside.

4   Heat 3 tbsp oil in a wok. Add finely chopped garlic and stir.

5   Add green chillies and stir. Add onions and capsicums. Cook for 2 minutes without stirring too much.

6   Remove from heat. Add all the remaining ingredients. Return to heat and stir for 2 minutes.

7   Add chicken. Mix & add cornflour paste. Stir for 2-3 minutes. Check seasonings. Add more soya sauce if you like a darker colour. Serve hot.

Soups and Salads

Chicken Stock for Soups

Makes 10 cups

½ kg chicken - cleaned and cut into pieces
1 onion - sliced, 1 tsp chopped garlic, 1 tsp chopped ginger
1 carrot - cut into pieces, 1 tsp salt, 12 cups of water

1   Put all the ingredients in a cooker. Pressure cook to allow one whistle. Keep on low heat for 5 minutes.

2   Cool and remove the meat from the bones. (This meat can be used in soups, fried rice, noodles).

3   Add the bones to the liquid in the cooker along with 1 cup of water & simply cook without pressure on low heat for another 15 minutes. Strain and use.

Note:
- Stock can be made in advance and frozen in the freezer compartment and used when required.
- **Quick Stock**—Soup cubes or stock cubes may be boiled with water and used instead of fresh stock.

Clear Chicken Soup

Serves 4

5 CUPS CLEAR CHICKEN STOCK
as given above

OTHER INGREDIENTS
1 cabbage leaf - cut into 1" squares
¼ carrot - cut into 2" long juliennes (¼ cup)
1-2 mushrooms - sliced very thinly, 2-3 spinach leaves - torn roughly
1 tsp tabasco sauce, 1 tsp worcestershire, ¼ tsp white pepper

1   Make stock as given above. Remove chicken from stock. Shred meat into thin broad strips from the bones. Cover and keep chicken aside. Return stock to fire with the bones and cook till reduced to half or about 5 cups. Remove from fire and strain stock through a very fine sieve or a muslin cloth.

2   Add spinach, cabbage, carrot juliennes and mushrooms to stock.

3   Add tabasco and worcestershire sauce. Boil. Add about ½ tsp salt and ¼ tsp white pepper to taste. Add the shredded chicken and bring to a boil. Serve.

Tom Yum Soup

Serves 4

PASTE (CRUSH TOGETHER)
½ tsp red chilli flakes, 1 tsp chopped garlic
1 tsp chopped ginger, ½ tsp salt

OTHER INGREDIENTS
1 tbsp oil
½ stalk lemon grass - cut into thin slices diagonally - see below
5 cups water
2 stock cubes - crushed
3 kaffir lime leaves - whole
1" piece galangal (Thai ginger) - cut into paper thin slices
1-2 baby corns - cut into paper thin slices
¼ cup very tiny florets of broccoli
½ small carrot - cut into paper thin slices
2 fresh or dry red chillies - sliced
2-3 tbsp lemon juice
2 tsp light soya sauce, ¾ tsp salt, ¼ tsp pepper, 2 tsp sugar

1 Prepare the paste by crushing all the ingredients of the paste.

2 In a deep pan, heat 1 tbsp oil. Add the above paste and lemon grass. Mix well.

3 Add water, lime leaves, sliced ginger, baby corn slices and the soup/stock cubes. You can knot the upper grass of lemon grass and put that also in the soup. After the boil, keep covered on low heat for 5 minutes.

4 Reduce heat. Add light soya sauce, salt, pepper and sugar to taste. Simmer for 1 minute.

5 Add mushrooms, carrots, broccoli and red chillies. Boil for 2 minutes on medium flame. Add lemon juice. Remove the kinot of lemon grass. Pour into individual bowls and serve hot.

About Lemon Grass

Only the lower stem of lemon grass is edible. The upper grass like portion has a lot of flavour but is not edible. So to use lemon grass, remove the grass portion. Discard 1" hard portion from the base of the stalk of lemon grass and then cut the stalk into thin slices. Tie the remaining grass portion into a knot. You can put this flavourful knot in the soup and discard it at serving time.

Yakhani Murg Shorba

Serves 8

500 gm chicken with bones - cut into pieces
2 onions - sliced thinly and deep fried till crisp & golden brown
1 tbsp melted butter, 3 tbsp chopped green coriander

GROUND MASALA PASTE
1 onion - finely chopped, 4 tbsp chopped garlic, 2" cinnamon (*dalchini*)
10 black peppercorns (*saboot kali mirch*), 1 tsp fennel (*saunf*) seeds
2 tsp coriander seeds (*saboot dhania*), 2 tsp salt or to taste

1. Grind onion and garlic with all the spices to a paste. Keep aside.

2. Place the chicken pieces in a pressure cooker with 8 cups of water and the ground masala paste. Pressure cook to give 2 whistles and simmer for 5 minutes. Remove from heat. Drop the pressure by placing the cooker under tap water.

3. Strain the soup in a soup strainer to get a clear stock or soup. Pick up the chicken pieces.

4. Separate the chicken pieces from the bones into small chicken shreds and keep aside.

5. Deep fry onion slices to a golden colour. Keep aside till serving time.

6. Add salt to taste, chicken shreds, chopped coriander leaves and melted butter to the clear chicken soup. Mix well.

7. At serving time, boil soup and add the fried onions. Bring to a boil and pour soup in individual bowls.

Chicken Almond Soup

Serves 4-5

4 cups chicken stock or 4 cups water boiled with 1 chicken stock cube

½ cup boiled and finely shredded chicken (from stock, page 50)

1 cup milk

1 tbsp butter

1 tbsp plain flour (*maida*)

8-10 almonds - crushed roughly

salt and pepper to taste

4 tbsp fresh cream to garnish

1   Mix the chicken stock and milk and keep aside.

2   Heat butter in a pan. Add the flour and almonds. Stir on low heat for 1 minute.

3   Add stock and milk mixture. Bring to a boil, stirring continuously. Cook on low heat until the soup thickens.

4   Add boiled chicken, salt and pepper. Cook for a minute. Serve hot, garnished with fresh cream, spring onion greens or coriander and some shredded almonds in each cup.

53

Chicken Minestrone

Serves 4-5

½ cup boiled and shredded chicken (from stock, page 50)

4 cups chicken stock or 4 cups water mixed with 2 stock cubes, see note

3 medium sized tomatoes - blanched, peeled and chopped finely

2 tbsp butter, 1 onion - chopped finely (½ cup)

1 small potato - diced into small pieces (½ cup)

1 carrot - diced into small pieces (½ cup)

3-4 tbsp finely chopped celery or green french beans

2-3 tbsp baked beans, see note, salt and pepper to taste

1. To blanch the tomatoes, put them in hot water for 10 minutes. Remove from water and peel them to remove skin. Chop them finely. Keep aside.

2. Heat butter. Add onion and fry till light brown.

3. Add celery, carrots and potatoes and stir fry for 1-2 minutes.

4. Add chopped tomatoes. Cook 2-3 minutes. Add stock and baked beans.

5. Give one boil. Lower heat. Cover and simmer for 20 minutes. Add salt and pepper to taste and mix well.

6. Add boiled chicken. Bring to a boil.

7. Serve hot, garnished with some grated cheese.

Note:

- The left over baked beans can be stored in a clean stainless steel or a plastic container in the freezer compartment of the refrigerator without getting spoilt for a month.

- Instead of stock (made at home), 4 cups water and 2 chicken soup cubes can be used. Do not add any salt, if using soup cubes as they already contain salt. Taste at the end and adjust salt to taste.

- Peas, zucchini, crushed garlic and chopped parsley can be used to give it a different flavour. Total amount of vegetables should not exceed 2-2½ cups.

Hot & Sour Chicken Soup

Serves 4

1 breast of chicken - shredded or cut into small pieces
1 tbsp oil, 1 tsp finely chopped garlic, 1 tsp red chilli paste
2 tbsp thinly sliced or shredded mushrooms
2 tbsp shredded bamboo shoots (optional)
4 tbsp shredded cabbage
3 tbsp carrot - shredded
green portion of 1 spring onion - finely chopped
5 cups chicken stock or 5 cups water mixed with 2 chicken soup cubes
2 tsp soya sauce, 2 tbsp vinegar, 1 tsp sugar
½ tsp ajinomoto (optional), ½ tsp black pepper
4 tbsp cornflour
1 egg - lightly beaten, salt to taste

1   Heat 1 tbsp oil in a pan. Add finely chopped garlic. Stir and add red chilli paste. Add shredded chicken and stir for 2-3 minutes till cooked.

2   Add the mushrooms, bamboo shoots, cabbage and carrot. Saute for 1 minute. Do not cook longer and keep the vegetables crunchy.

3   Add the stock and give it 2-3 boils. Reduce heat and add soya sauce, vinegar, sugar, ajinomoto and pepper.

4   Add spring onion leaves. Mix cornflour with ½ cup water. Add to the soup, stirring constantly.

5   Bring to a boil. Gradually pour in lightly beaten egg, stirring the soup continuously with a fork to get shreds of egg. Check salt and vinegar add if required. Mix. Remove from fire. Serve hot.

Manchow Soup

Serves 4

6 cups chicken stock, 1 tbsp oil

1 tbsp finely chopped garlic

¾ cup boiled and shredded chicken (from stock, page 50)

2 baby corns - very finely chopped (¼ cup)

¼ cup very finely chopped cabbage

¼ cup very finely chopped carrot

½ tsp salt, ½ tsp pepper, or to taste

1½-2 tsp soya sauce

4-5 tbsp cornflour dissolved in ½ cup stock

1 tbsp spring onion greens to garnish, optional

1   In a wok, heat oil. Add garlic and fry till it turns brownish.

2   Add finely chopped vegetables and fry for 1 minute.

3   Add stock. Bring to a boil. Add salt, pepper and soya sauce.

4   Add cornflour paste and cook stirring till it boils. Simmer for 2-3 minutes.

5   Add boiled chicken. Boil again. Serve hot in soup bowls topped with greens.

Hawaiian Chicken Salad

Serves 4

250 gm boneless chicken or 2 chicken breasts - cut into thin strips
1 tsp lemon juice, 1 tbsp oil, 3 slices of pineapple - cut into 1" pieces
½ onion - shredded or sliced - keep in a bowl of cold water in the fridge
½ carrot - cut into juliennes
½ cup shredded cabbage - keep in cold water in the fridge
8-10 tender french beans - keep whole or cut into 2 pieces
salt and pepper to taste

DRESSING
8 tbsp mayonnaise, ½ tsp pepper, 2 tbsp water
2½ tbsp hot & sweet tomato sauce

1. Place chicken in a pressure cooker with ½ cup water, 1 tbsp oil, 1 tsp lemon juice & ¼ tsp salt, pressure cook to 1-2 whistles. Keep on low heat for 1 minute. Remove from heat. When the pressure drops, drain chicken. You can also microwave the chicken by placing the chicken mixed with the oil, salt and lemon juice in a flat micro proof flat dish in a single layer. Cover with a wrap and microwave for 3 minutes. Check after 5 minutes for doneness.

2. String french beans. Boil 4 cups water with ½ tsp salt, 1 tsp lemon juice and 1 tsp sugar. Add beans. Boil for 1 minute. Strain and refresh in cold water.

3. Mix all ingredients of the dressing in a bowl. Add chicken and beans. Mix well. Chill in the fridge till serving time.

4. At serving time, drain and pat dry vegetables on a clean napkin. Mix vegetables and pineapple to the chicken in dressing. Chill for 10 minutes. Serve.

Greek Chicken Salad

Serves 6

1 chicken breast (150 gm) boneless chicken - cut widthwise into thin strips

100 gm feta cheese or *paneer* - cut into ½" square pieces

3 onions - sliced, 2 red capsicums - sliced

2 yellow or green capsicums - sliced

1 cucumber (*kheera*) - cut into half moons (1½ cups)

½ cup sliced black olives, 4 tomatoes - sliced

DRESSING

1½ cups yogurt (*dahi*), 2 tsp mustard sauce, 3 tbsp lemon juice

2 tbsp grated lemon rind (see note), 3 flakes garlic - crushed

2 tbsp chopped mint (*poodina*), ½ tsp salt or to taste, ½ tsp pepper

1. Boil 4 cups water with ½ tsp salt and 1 tsp lemon juice. Add chicken strips. Boil for 2 minutes or till chicken turns tender. Remove from water. Keep aside.

2. To make half moons of the cucumber, remove bitterness of the cucumber. Peel. Cut lengthwise into two halves. With the help of a scooper or the back of a teaspoon, remove the seeds from the cucumber by pulling the spoon straight down the length of the cucumber half. This way you get a groove in the cucumber piece. Cut the cucumber into ¼" thick, half-moon slices.

3. For the dressing, mix yogurt, mustard, lemon juice, rind, garlic, mint, salt and pepper. Taste and adjust the seasonings.

4. In the serving bowl, mix chicken and cucumber with the rest of ingredients. Spoon dressing over and toss lightly to serve.

Note:
- For lemon rind — Wash and dry 1 lemon. Grate gently on a grater to remove the upper yellow skin, the lemon rind.

Caesar Salad

Serves 4

½ bunch lettuce leaves (50 gm) preferably iceberg variety

1 chicken breast (125 gm)

1 large tomato - deseeded & cut into thin long pieces

STIR FRIED GARLIC CROUTONS

2 slices of 1 day old white bread, 2 tsp butter

2-3 flakes garlic - crushed, 4-6 peppercorns (*saboot kali mirch*) - crushed

DRESSING

2 tbsp vinegar, preferably balsamic vinegar

1 tbsp lemon juice, 2 flakes garlic - crushed finely

6 tbsp olive oil, ¾ tsp salt, ¼ tsp black pepper powder

1 tsp sugar, 1 tsp mustard sauce

GARNISH (OPTIONAL)

2 tbsp cheese, preferably parmesan

1. Prick chicken breast. Sprinkle salt, pepper, 1 tbsp oil and 1 tsp lemon juice. Keep aside for 15 minutes.

2. Place the chicken breast in a pressure cooker with ½ cup water and ¼ tsp salt. Pressure cook to give 1 whistle and then remove from heat. Cool. Cut the breast into slices and keep in a bowl.

3. Wash the lettuce. Tear the leaves into smaller pieces. Soak in chilled water.

4. Mix all ingredients of the dressing in a small bottle or mixer and shake well.

5. Pour dressing over the chicken pieces in the bowl. Mix well. Cover & refrigerate.

6. To make croutons, mix butter with garlic and peppercorns and spread on one side of the slice. Remove the sides of the bread and cut into small cubes. Brown them in an ungreased non stick pan over medium heat for 5-7 minutes, stirring frequently, till golden brown. Remove from pan and keep aside.

7. At serving time, wipe dry the lettuce leaves in a clean kitchen towel to drain out water.

8. Mix lettuce leaves, tomatoes and croutons in a large salad bowl. Pour the dressing along with the chicken pieces on the vegetables etc. Toss gently with a fork. Garnish with cheese. Serve.

Thousand Island Tomatoes

Serves 8

1 chicken breast, 8 small tomatoes
2 canned pineapple slices
2 tbsp shredded green or red cabbage

THOUSAND ISLAND DRESSING
3 tbsp mayonnaise, 1 tbsp thick cream
1 tbsp ready made tomato puree, a few drops of tabasco sauce
¼ tsp pepper, salt to taste, 1 tsp very finely chopped onion
1 tsp very finely chopped capsicum

1 Wash chicken. Prick chicken with a fork. Pressure cook with ½ tsp salt and ½ cup water to give 2 whistles. Debone the meat & shred it into small pieces.

2 Wash and dry tomatoes. Cut a slice from the top & scoop out the pulp carefully.

3 Sprinkle salt and pepper inside the tomato. Rub the salt inside. Keep them upside down.

4 Cut pineapple slices in small pieces. Squeeze gently to remove excess syrup.

5 Mix pineapple pieces, shredded chicken and cabbage in a bowl.

6 Mix together - mayonnaise, cream, tomato puree, tabasco, salt and pepper to taste. Add chopped onion and capsicum also.

7 Pour the dressing over the chicken. Mix. Fill the tomatoes with the mixture.

8 Decorate on a bed of salad leaves. Serve chilled.

Smoked Chicken Salad

Serves 6

2 tbsp olive oil, 4 chicken breasts - cut into long strips

2 spring onions - sliced diagonally including the greens

1 red capsicum (*red pepper*) - cut into ¼" wide strips

1 small red or green chilli - deseeded and finely sliced diagonally

1 tbsp chopped fresh coriander

ORANGE AND GINGER DRESSING

4 tbsp orange juice, 2 tsp finely grated fresh ginger, 6 tbsp olive oil

3 tbsp white vinegar, 2 tbsp white wine, 1½ tsp brown sugar

½ tsp salt, ½ tsp pepper, or to taste

TO SMOKE CHICKEN

5-6 pieces of burning coal (get from your *press waala*)

2 tsp dry parsley or thyme, 1 tsp oil

1. Wash chicken. Pat dry. Cut into strips. Place a small steel bowl or a *katori* in a deep pan or a kadhai with a lid. Put the chicken around the steel bowl. Place the coal pieces on the naked flame for 5-7 minutes, till they turn grey and red hot at the edges. Put burning coal pieces in the steel bowl. Sprinkle herbs on the burning coal. Pour some oil on the coal and cover chicken immediately to trap the smoke. Leave covered for 10 minutes for the chicken to acquire a smoky flavour.

2. Heat 2 tbsp oil in a *kadhai* or a pan. Add smoked chicken and cook on medium heat, stirring continuously otherwise the chicken will stick to the pan. Fry for 3-4 minutes till chicken turns whitish and light golden from various sides. Remove chicken from fire when cooked.

3. Place smoked chicken, spring onions, red capsicum, chilli and coriander in a serving bowl.

4. To make dressing, place all ingredients of the dressing in a mixer. Blend for few seconds.

5. Pour the prepared dressing over the chicken mixture and mix well to combine. Cover with a plastic wrap or a plate and chill till serving time. To serve, mix well with two forks and serve cold.

Cold Cuts with Greens

Serves 4

100 gm chicken salami (12-14 pieces), 100 gm ham (5-6 pieces)

8-10 leaves of ice berg lettuce, 8-10 rocket leaves or small spinach leaves

8-10 leaves of leafy lettuce

10-15 green olives stuffed with pimentos - halved

DRESSING

6 tbsp extra virgin olive oil, 2 tbsp white vinegar

½ tsp garlic paste, 1 tsp honey, ½ tsp mustard powder/paste (1 tsp)

½ tsp each of salt, pepper, oregano

1   Break lettuce leaves with the hand. Keep rocket or spinach leaves whole. Dip leaves in cold water for 15 minutes.

2   Cut cold meat into ½" broad slices, about 1-2" long.

3   Mix all ingredients of the dressing in a screw top jar. Shake well.

4   Remove leaves from water. Pat on a towel lightly to absorb excess moisture.

5   To serve, mix leaves and cold cuts. Drizzle dressing. Toss well. Transfer to a serving platter. Top with olives.

Mexican Chicken Salad

Serves 4-5

300 gm chicken with bones, 1 tbsp oil
¾ cup baked beans in tomato sauce (available in tins)
½ cup chopped red capsicum, ½ cup chopped yellow capsicum
½ cup chopped cucumber, 3-4 lettuce leaves (iceberg or regular lettuce)

DRESSING
1-2 green chillies (depending on taste) or 1 tbsp chopped jalapenos
4 tbsp lemon juice, 4 tbsp olive oil or salad oil
2 tsp cumin (*jeera*) seeds, 2 tsp oregano, 1¼ tsp salt

1   To boil chicken, put chicken, 1 tbsp oil, ¼ tsp salt and ½ cup water in a pressure cooker. Pressure cook to give 2 whistles. Remove from fire. Let the pressure drop by itself. Cool and debone and shred chicken.

2   Grind all the ingredients written under dressing in a mixer till well blended.

3   In a bowl mix together - beans, cucumber, red-yellow capsicum and boiled chicken. Pour dressing over the salad and mix well. Chill till serving time.

4   In a serving plate arrange lettuce at the base of the dish. Chill in the refrigerator till serving time. To serve, mix the chilled salad with two forks and spread over the arranged lettuce leaves.

Julienne Chicken Sausage Salad

Serves 4-6

6 chicken sausages
1 tsp oil, 6 baby corns, 6-8 button mushrooms, 1 tsp lemon juice
½ green capsicum, ½ yellow capsicum, 1 firm tomato

DRESSING
6 tbsp olive oil
2 tbsp vinegar, ½ tsp salt, ½ tsp pepper, ½ tsp powdered sugar
1 tsp mustard sauce, 1 tbsp chopped parsley/cilantro
2-3 flakes garlic - crushed & chopped

1. Heat 1 tsp oil in a non-stick pan. Saute sausages for 1-2 minutes till light golden. Remove from heat. Cut diagonally into ¼" thick slices. Keep aside.

2. Deseed capsicums and cut into strips. Cut tomato into 4 pieces lengthwise, remove the pulp and cut into thin strips.

3. Boil 4 cups water with 1 tsp salt and 1 tsp lemon juice. Add baby corns and mushrooms to the boiling water. Remove from heat after 1 minute. Strain the blanched vegetables.

4. Pat dry vegetables on a clean kitchen towel. Slice baby corns diagonally, cut each mushroom into four pieces.

5. Mix sausages, mushrooms, baby corns, capsicums & tomato in a salad bowl.

6. Mix all the ingredients of the dressing with a whisk, till it gets thick and emulsified.

7. Pour the dressing over the salad mixture in the bowl. Mix well and keep aside to chill in the fridge till serving time. Mix once again before serving.

Pasta Chicken Salad

Serves 4-6

2 chicken breasts
1 tbsp oil
1 cup uncooked macaroni or any other pasta
1 capsicum - chopped, 3 tbsp olive oil or any cooking oil
½ cup tomato puree (ready-made)
2 tbsp tomato ketchup, ½ tsp red chilli sauce, ¼ tsp sugar, salt to taste
few drops tabasco sauce, 1 tsp dried oregano
2-3 tbsp chopped parsley or coriander, 2-3 tbsp fresh cream
lettuce leaves and capsicum to garnish

1   Boil 3-4 cups of water with 1 tsp of salt and 1 tsp of oil. Add macaroni or any other pasta to the boiling water. Cook for 7-8 minutes till soft. Leave macaroni in hot water for 1-2 minutes and then strain. Wash several times with cold water. Sprinkle 1 tbsp oil and keep aside.

2   To boil chicken, add ½ cup of water in a pressure cooker with ¼ tsp of salt, 1 tbsp oil and chicken. Pressure cook to give 2 whistles. Cool and cube (size of macaroni) the cooked chicken.

3   Heat 2 tbsp oil in a nonstick pan. Add tomato puree. Stir for ½ minute. Add the tomato sauce, red chilli sauce and ½ cup of water. Simmer the sauce on low flame for a few seconds till slightly thick.

4   Add salt, sugar, tabasco, oregano and parsley. Remove from fire. Add cream.

5   Mix the cooked pasta, chicken and capsicum in a bowl. Pour the sauce over it and cover and keep in a refrigerator for ½ hour.

6   Before serving, arrange some lettuce leaves on a serving platter. If the salad gets a little dry (as pasta absorbs water) add a few tablespoons water to get a slightly wet consistency. Transfer the macaroni salad on the lettuce leaves.

7   Cut the capsicum into thin rings. Half the rings, deseed them and arrange on the edges. Serve cold.

Indian

Murg Nizam

Serves 6-7

800 gm chicken - cut into 12 pieces, 8 tbsp oil or ghee
2 onions - chopped, 3 tbsp ginger paste, 3 tbsp garlic paste
8 green chillies - deseeded & chopped, 1 tsp turmeric (*haldi*), 2½ tsp salt
¼ cup peanuts & 2 tbsp melon seeds (*magaz*) - crushed coarsely
2/3 cup coconut - brown skin removed and grated
¾ cup yogurt - whisked till smooth
1 tsp garam masala, 1 tbsp lemon juice
1/3 cup chopped green coriander, 1/3 cup chopped mint (*poodina*)

1   Heat oil and add onions and saute over medium heat until golden brown. Add the ginger and garlic pastes, stir for a minute. Add green chillies, salt and turmeric. Mix.

2   Add the crushed peanuts and melon seeds, grated coconut, stir for a minute.

3   Add yogurt & bhuno for 3-4 minutes. Now add chicken, Bhuno for 3-4 minutes. Add about 1½ cups water, bring to a boil, simmer for 15-20 minutes, or until tender. Adjust the seasoning.

4   Sprinkle garam masala, lemon juice, coriander, mint and toasted melon seeds. Remove to a dish and serve with nan or parantha.

Murgh Malai Korma

Serves 6

800 gm boneless chicken - cut into 1" pieces
4 tomatoes, 2 tsp watermelon seeds (*magaz*)
½ cup oil, 2 tsp finely chopped, 2 tbsp chopped garlic
2 green chillies - chopped, 2 cups yogurt, 1½ cups fresh cream
1 tsp salt or to taste

GRIND TOGETHER IN A SMALL SPICE GRINDER
½ tsp peppercorn (*saboot kali mirch*), 1 tsp cumin (*jeera*) seeds
10 almonds - chopped, a pinch of grated nutmeg (*jaiphal*)
¼ tsp or a blade of mace (*javitri*), 1 tsp coriander seeds (*saboot dhania*)
2 green cardamoms (*chhoti elaichi*), ½" stick cinnamon (*dalchini*)

1. Boil 3-4 cups water. Put whole tomatoes in boiling water & boil for 3-4 minutes till the skin starts to peel. Remove from water. After they cool down, peel and chop roughly.

2. Grind the tomatoes with watermelon seeds, ginger, garlic, green chillies in a mixer till smooth. Add yogurt to the mixer and blend again to mix the yogurt well with the tomatoes.

3. Heat ½ cup oil in a kadhai and add the prepared tomato-yogurt puree. Stir on medium flame and bring to a boil. Add chicken pieces and salt. Cook without covering on low heat, stirring occasionally till chicken is tender. Add about ¼ cup water if required.

4. When the chicken is tender, add the spices and the almonds ground together. Reduce heat and cook for 2-3 minutes. Add the cream and mix gently. Serve hot.

Rajasthani Chicken Curry

Serves 6

1 kg chicken - cut into pieces
8 tbsp oil
2" stick cinnamon (*dalchini*), seeds of 4 green cardamom (*chhoti elaichi*)
2 onions - cut into thin slices, 1½ tbsp ginger-garlic paste
1 tsp turmeric (*haldi*) powder, 2 tsp salt or to taste
6 whole, dry red chillies - crushed, 4 tomatoes - pureed in a mixer
½ cup yogurt - whisked, 2 tbsp green coriander - finely chopped

1   Marinate chicken with salt. Keep aside for 10 minutes.

2   Heat oil in a pan & sauté chicken in batches till they turn brown. Keep aside.

3   In the same oil, add cinnamon stick and cardamom seeds, wait for a minute.

4   Add onions and sauté till golden brown.

5   Add ginger-garlic paste and sauté for 2 minutes, add turmeric powder and crushed red chillies.

6   Add freshly pureed tomatoes and stir fry till dry and oil separates.

7   Add 2 cups water and cook till tomatoes are well blended in the gravy. Check salt and adjust.

8   Add stir fried chicken pieces, cover and cook on low heat for 15-20 minutes. Remove from fire.

9   Let chicken cool slightly and put yogurt and mix well. Heat if required.

10 Garnish with coriander and serve with rice.

Butter Chicken

Serves 4

MARINATE TOGETHER

1 medium sized chicken (800 gm) - cut into 12 pieces

½ cup yogurt - hang for 45 minutes in a muslin cloth, 1 tbsp garlic paste

1 tbsp dry fenugreek leaves (*kasoori methi*)

½ tsp black salt (*kala namak)*, 1 tsp garam masala

MAKHANI GRAVY

Boil Together

½ kg (6-7) tomatoes - roughly chopped

½" piece ginger, 10 flakes garlic - finely chopped, 2 green chillies -chop

5-6 cloves (*laung*), 4-5 green cardamoms (*chhoti elaichi*) - pounded to open

1½ tsp degi mirch, 2 cups water

Add later to the gravy

2 tbsp oil, 2 tbsp butter, 1 tsp ginger-garlic paste

1 tsp kashmiri red chilli (*degi mirch*), 2 tbsp butter, ¼ cup cream,

4 tbsp cashewnuts (*kaju*) - soak in ¼ cup hot water for 15 min, grind to

a smooth paste, ½ tsp garam masala, 1 tsp salt, or to taste

2 tsp tandoori masala (optional), ¼ tsp sugar or to taste

1 tbsp dry fenugreek leaves (*kasoori methi*) - dry roasted on a *tawa* for

2 minutes and crushed to a powder, pinch of orange colour

1. Wash and pat dry chicken. For the marinade, mix hung yogurt, garlic paste, dry fenugreek leaves, black salt, garam masala & colour. Rub the chicken with this mixture. Keep aside for 30 mins or preferably overnight in the fridge.

2. Heat 6 tbsp oil in a kadhai, add marinated chicken, cook on high heat for 5-6 minutes, stirring all the time. Reduce heat and cook covered for about 10 minutes or till tender. Add ½ tsp salt. Mix well. Remove from fire. Keep aside.

3. To prepare the makhani gravy, boil tomatoes with all the ingredients. Reduce heat and cook covered on low heat for 15 minutes till slightly reduced in quantity. Remove from fire. Cool completely for 15 minutes. Grind to a smooth puree. Strain puree through a metal strainer.

4. Heat 2 tbsp oil and 2 tbsp butter in a kadhai. Add 1 tsp ginger-garlic paste and stir till golden. Add 1 tsp degi mirch. Stir and add prepared tomato puree. Boil. Cook for 5-7 minutes. Add all the remaining ingredients of the gravy. Bring to a boil, stirring continuously. Cook on medium heat till you get the desired colour and thickness of the gravy. Add a pinch of colour if needed. Add cooked chicken. Simmer for 2 minutes till the gravy turns to a bright colour. Garnish with 1 tbsp of fresh cream and slit green chillies. Serve hot.

Kasoori Murg

Serves 4-6

1 medium sized chicken (800 gm) - cut into 12 pieces
¾ cup thick yogurt, salt to taste
4-5 tbsp oil
2 dry, red chillies - broken into pieces
3 large onions - chopped finely
2 tbsp finely chopped garlic
2 tbsp finely chopped ginger
2 green chillies - finely chopped
1 tsp coriander (*dhania*) powder
½ tsp red chilli powder
2 tomatoes - finely chopped
4 tbsp dry fenugreek leaves (*kasoori methi*)

(SABOOT MASALA) WHOLE GARAM MASALA
1 brown cardamom (*moti illaichi*)
2 green cardamoms (*chhoti illaichi*)
1" stick cinnamon (*dalchini*)
3-4 cloves (*laung*)
1 bay leaf (*tej patta*)

1 Marinate chicken with yogurt and salt. Keep aside to marinate for 30 minutes.

2 Heat oil in a heavy bottomed pan. Reduce flame, add broken chillies, chopped onions and all the whole garam masalas. Stir fry on medium heat until the onions turn golden brown.

3 Add chopped ginger and garlic. Stir for a minute. Reduce heat.

4 Add green chillies, red chilli powder and coriander powder. Mix.

5 Add tomatoes, stir fry till oil separates or tomatoes turn soft.

6 Add chicken. Stir fry for 2 minutes on high flame and then lower heat.

7 Cover and cook, stirring occasionally, till the chicken is tender and masala coats the chicken. Sprinkle some water in-between if needed.

8 Add the dry fenugreek leaves. Stir to mix. Garnish with ginger match sticks and coriander leaves.

Saag Murg

Serves 4

½ kg chicken with bones - cut into 5-6 pieces

2 tbsp oil, 1 tbsp ginger garlic paste, 1 onion - chopped

CURRY

600 - 700 gm spinach (*paalak*), choose a bundle with smaller leaves

2 onions - chopped, ½ tsp cumin (*jeera*) seeds

1½ tsp garlic paste (5-6 flakes of garlic - crushed to a paste)

¾ tsp cinnamon (*dalchini*) powder, ½ tsp garam masala

¼ tsp red chilli powder, ¾ coriander powder (*dhania*), ½ tsp salt

¼ tsp dry mango powder (*amchoor*)

2 tomatoes - chopped, 1 green chilli - chopped

1 tbsp dried fenugreek leaves (*kasoori methi*), 3-4 tbsp cream (optional)

BAGHAR (TEMPERING)

1 tbsp ghee or butter, 1" piece ginger - cut into thin long pieces (juliennes)

1 green chilli - slit into long pieces, ½ tsp red chilli powder

1. Chop spinach leaves, discarding the stalks. (Wash leaves in several changes of water. Hold a small bunch on the chopping board, then holding the bunch tightly, cut off the hard stems and then start cutting the leaves finely.)

2. For curry, heat 3 tbsp oil in a kadhai. Add cumin, onions and garlic. Cook till light brown.

3. Add cinnamon powder, garam masala, red chilli powder, coriander powder, amchoor and salt. Stir on low flame for 1 minute.

4. Add chopped tomatoes. Cook for 3-4 minutes, till well blended.

5. Add spinach and green chilli. Cook uncovered for 5-7 minutes on low flame. Remove from fire. Cool.

6. Blend the cooled mixture along with ½ cup water, just for a few seconds, to a coarse paste. Do not grind it too finely. Keep aside.

7. Heat oil in another *kadhai*, add onion cook till golden brown. Add chicken and ginger-garlic paste, bhuno for 10-15 minutes, stirring continuously.

8. Add the prepared green paste and dried fenugreek leaves. Mix well and cook covered on low heat for 4-5 minutes.

9. Add 1 cup milk and ½ cup water. Give it one boil. Simmer for 2-3 minutes. Add cream. Mix. Check salt and remove from fire.

10. Transfer to a serving dish. Heat 1 tbsp desi ghee or butter. Add ginger and green chilli. Remove from fire. Add red chilli powder and pour ghee on paalak.

Chicken Tikka Masala

Serves 4

200-250 gm cooked chicken tikka - (prepare chicken tikka as given on page 35)

2 cloves (*laung*) and seeds of 2 green cardamoms (*chhoti elaichi*) - crushed together, ½ tsp chat masala

MASALA

3 tbsp oil

½ tsp carom seeds (*ajwain*), ½ tsp onion seeds (*kalonji*)

2 onions - sliced finely, 1 tsp chopped ginger, 1 tbsp garlic paste

2-3 green chillies - deseeded and finely chopped

2 tsp coriander (*dhania*) powder, 1 tsp degi mirch

¼ tsp turmeric (*haldi*) powder, 1 tsp ground cumin (*jeera*)

2 tomatoes - chopped, 4 tbsp ready-made tomato puree

1½ tbsp dry fenugreek leaves (*kasuri methi*) - roast on a tawa for 2 minutes on low heat and crush to a powder

4 tbsp coriander - finely chopped, ½ tsp salt, ½ tsp garam masala

a pinch of sugar, 1 tbsp butter, 1 tbsp cream, optional

1 Prepare chicken tikka as given on page 35.

2 Heat 5 tbsp oil, add carom seeds and onion seeds. Wait for 1 minute.

3 Add onions. Stir fry till golden brown. Add green chillies, ginger and garlic. Saute over medium heat for 1-2 minutes.

4 Add coriander powder, degi mirch, turmeric powder and cumin powder. Stir till onions turn golden brown.

5 Add tomatoes and tomato puree. Cook for about 5 minutes till oil separates.

6 Add salt, dry fenugreek leaves, powdered cloves and green cardamoms. Mix well.

7 Add the cooked chicken tikka to the masala. Add 1 tbsp butter. Mix well.

8 Add chopped coriander, garam masala, sugar and chat masala. Mix well. Check salt and add as needed. Add cream if you like. Serve hot.

Chicken Chettinad

Serves 4-6

1 chicken (700-800 gm) - cut into 12 pieces, 5-6 tbsp oil
1 large onion - chopped very finely, ¼ cup curry leaves (*curry patta*)
3 tomatoes - pureed in a mixer, 1 tsp salt, or to taste
¼ tsp turmeric (*haldi*) powder, ¼ tsp chilli powder, 2-3 tbsp lemon juice
1 tbsp poppy seeds (*khus khus*)
2 tbsp cashewnuts (*kaju*) - broken pieces
1 cup milk, 2-3" piece ginger, 8-10 flakes garlic

CHETTINAD MASALA
½ cup freshly grated coconut (remove brown skin before grating)
1 tsp coriander seeds (*saboot dhania*)
1 tsp fennel seeds (*saunf*), ½ tsp cumin seeds (*jeera*)
2½ tsp peppercorns (*saboot kali mirch*)
5-6 whole, dry red chillies
3 green cardamoms (*chhoti illaichi*), 2-3 cloves (*laung*)
1" cinnamon stick (*dalchini*), 1 tbsp oil

1 Soak poppy seeds and cashewnuts in a little warm water for 10-15 minutes.

2 Heat 1 tbsp oil in a pan or *tawa*. Add coconut, coriander seeds, fennel seeds, cumin, peppercorns, dry red chillies, seeds of green cardamoms, cloves and cinnamon to oil. Stir-fry till fragrant. Remove from fire.

3 Drain poppy seeds and cashews. Grind together the roasted masala with the drained poppy seeds-cashewnuts, ginger and garlic in a mixer grinder to a very smooth paste with ¼ cup water. Keep aside.

4 Grind tomatoes in a mixer to a smooth puree. Keep aside.

5 Heat oil in a *kadhai* and add the chopped onions. Fry till light brown.

6 Add the chicken and cook or bhuno for 10 minutes.

7 Add the pureed tomatoes, salt, turmeric and chilli powder. Cook till tomatoes are well blended with the masala and oil separates.

8 Add the ground paste and curry leaves. Saute for 2 minutes.

9 Add lemon juice and 3 cups hot water. Cover and cook for 5-7 minutes or till chicken is tender, stirring in between. Cook till the masala is thick. Keep aside till serving time.

10 At serving time, add 1 cup milk to the chicken. Keep on low heat, stirring continuously, till it boils. Serve garnished with coriander.

Murg Mussalam

Serves 8

1 chicken (about 750 gm), you must buy a very small chicken broiler

MARINADE (GRIND TOGETHER)

1 cup yogurt (*dahi*), 10-12 flakes of garlic, 1" piece ginger, 2 green chillies

1" piece of raw papaya (*kachha papita*), ½ tsp red chilli powder

½ tsp garam masala, 1½ tsp salt, ½ tsp turmeric

SPICES - ROAST TOGETHER FOR MASALA

1 tbsp coriander seeds (*saboot dhania*), 6 cloves (*laung*)

6 peppercorns (*saboot kali mirch*), ½ tsp cumin (*jeera*) seeds

1" piece cinnamon (*dalchini*), seeds of 2 black cardamoms (*moti elaichi*)

1 tbsp desiccated coconut (*bura*)

2 tbsp almonds - blanched, put in hot water for 15 minutes, peel the skin and chop

a small blade of mace (*javitri*), a pinch of grated nutmeg (*jaiphal*)

OTHER INGREDIENTS FOR MASALA

6-8 tbsp oil, 4 onions - chopped, 6 flakes garlic - chopped

1" piece ginger, 1 tsp salt, ½ tsp red chilli powder, ¼ tsp garam masala

1½ cups water, ¼ tsp saffron (*kesar*) dissolved in 1 tbsp hot water

3 to 4 drops of kewra essence

GARNISH

1 tbsp chopped fresh coriander leaves

½ tsp saffron - soaked in 2 tbsp cream

1   Clean the chicken thoroughly and prick all over with a fork, make cuts over the breast and the legs if it is a little tough.

2   Grind the above-mentioned ingredients for the marinade into a fine paste.

3   Rub the ground paste into the chicken, all over the surface and the cavity. Leave chicken with this marinade for about 2 hours. Keep in the fridge.

4   To prepare the masala, lightly roast all spices together, given under spices, on low flame until fragrant. Do not make them brown. Remove from fire.

5   Heat 6-8 tbsp oil in a big kadhai (big enough to accommodate the whole chicken later). Add chopped onions and garlic. Do not add ginger. Remove onion and garlic from oil when they turn brown.

6   Grind all the roasted spices, browned onions and fresh ginger into a fine paste with a little water if required. Add salt, red chilli powder and garam masala to the paste. Keep the ground masala paste aside.

7. Heat left over oil, add ½ tsp red chilli powder. Stir and immediately add the marinated chicken and the left over marinade also. Cook for about 10-15 minutes till yogurt dries up and the chicken turns brown.

8. After it is done, add the ground masala paste (prepared above, step 6) Add 1½ cups water. Cook chicken covered on medium heat till tender, about 40 minutes. Turn the chicken after 20 minutes. Sprinkle some hot water over the chicken if the water dries while cooking.

9. Mix the dissolved saffron in 1 tbsp hot water with the essence and sprinkle over the chicken when it is nearly cooked. Cook for about 5 minutes more or till a thick gravy remains and oil separates.

10. To serve, heat chicken. Transfer to an oval dish. Pour the saffron soaked in cream on the chicken. Sprinkle coriander and garam masala powder.

Chicken Curry

Serves 4-5

1 medium size chicken with bones (700-800 gm) - cut into 12 pieces, wash and pat dry

10 tbsp oil, 1 bay leaf

4 cloves (*laung*), 1" stick cinnamon (*dalchini*)

4 black cardamoms (*moti illaichi*)

4 tomatoes - puree in a mixer

1½ tsp salt, or to taste

½ tsp red chilli powder

2 tbsp coriander (*dhania*) powder, ½ tsp turmeric (*haldi*) powder

1 tsp garam masala

½ cup thick yogurt - well beaten

2 tbsp chopped coriander (*dhania*)

GRIND TO A PASTE IN A MIXER

5 large onions, 1½" piece of ginger and 10-12 flakes of garlic

1. Sprinkle chicken with some salt & red chilli powder. Keep aside for 30 minutes.

2. Grind onion and ginger-garlic to a paste in a mixer. Puree tomatoes separately in a mixer and keep aside.

3. Heat oil in a heavy bottomed kadhai. Add the bay leaf, cloves, cinnamin and black cardamoms. Wait for a few seconds.

4. Add onion-ginger paste. Stir fry on medium heat till well browned.

5. Put the chicken pieces, bhuno nicely for 5-7 minutes on medium heat till the water evaporates and the chicken turns whitish first and then later it turns golden and glossy (The chicken leaves its own fat).

6. Add salt, red chillies, coriander powder, turmeric powder and garam masala. Stir for 2-3 minutes.

7. Add the freshly pureed tomatoes and 1 tsp coriander leaves. Cook for about 8-10 minutes. Stir after every few minutes. Cook till oil separates and the tomatoes blend well with the onions.

8. Reduce heat and add the yogurt. Bhuno for 3-4 minutes more, till the yogurt dries completely and oil separates.

9. Add about 2 cups of water. Boil. Cover and cook on low heat for 5 minutes till the chicken turns tender and you get a nice masala gravy. Remove from fire and serve hot garnished with remaining coriander.

Chicken Jalfrezi

Serves 4

2 chicken breasts, 1 tsp lemon juice

1 large carrot - cut diagonally into thin slices

5-6 beans - cut diagonally into thin slices

½ green capsicum - deseed and cut into thin fingers

½ yellow or red pepper (capsicum) - deseeded & sliced into thin fingers

1 long, firm tomato - cut into 4, pulp removed & cut into thin long pieces

1 tbsp ginger-garlic paste or 2 tsp ginger-garlic - finely chopped

15-20 curry leaves

COLLECT TOGETHER

1 tsp cumin (*jeera*) seeds, ½ tsp mustard seeds

¾ tsp onion seeds (*kalonji*), ¼ tsp fenugreek seeds (*methi daana*)

MIX TOGETHER

½ cup tomato puree, 1 tbsp tomato ketchup

½ tsp red chilli powder

1 tsp coriander (*dhania*) powder, ½ tsp salt or to taste, ½ tsp sugar

1. Wash the chicken. Boil with ½ tsp salt and 1 tbsp oil in 1 cup water till tender or pressure cook to give 1 whistle. Keep the chicken stock aside.

2. Cut the chicken into thin strips widthwise. Sprinkle a pinch of salt and 1 tsp lemon juice. Mix.

3. Cut beans and carrots diagonally.

4. Put carrots and beans in salted boiling water for 2 minutes till crisp-tender. Strain and keep aside.

5. Mix together - tomato puree, tomato ketchup, red chilli powder, amchoor, coriander powder and salt in a bowl. Keep aside.

6. Collect all seeds written under collect together in a bowl.

7. Heat 4 tbsp oil in a kadhai. Add the collected seeds together. When cumin turns golden, reduce heat and add ginger-garlic and stir till golden. Add curry leaves and stir for a few seconds.

8. Add the tomato puree mixed with dry masalas and stir on medium heat for 2-3 minutes or till oil separates.

9. Add chicken strips and stir for 2 minutes.

10. Add carrots and beans. Stir for 1 minute. Add the capsicums and tomato. Add ¾ cup stock. Boil. Stir till well blended. Remove from fire.

Haryali Murg

Serves 6-8

1 chicken (700-800 gm) - cut into 12 pieces
500 gm spinach (*paalak*), 250 gm fenugreek greens (*methi*)
2-3 onions - chopped finely
3 tbsp ginger-garlic-green chilli paste
1 large tomato - chopped
½ cup thick yogurt - beaten well till smooth
1 tsp garam masala, 1 tsp chilli powder, salt to taste
½ cup milk or water
4-5 tbsp oil
2 tbsp cream to garnish (optional)

1 Discard stems of spinach and chop the leaves finely. Wash leaves in plenty of water, changing water several times.

2 Wash the fenugreek leaves in the same way. Sprinkle little salt and squeeze to remove bitterness from the leaves. Keep aside.

3 Heat oil in a heavy bottomed pan. Add onions. Cook till light brown.

4 Add the ginger-garlic paste. Cook for 1 minute.

5 Add tomato. Cook for 1 minute, till it turns mushy. Add yogurt, salt, chilli powder, garam masala and cook on high flame or till oil separates a little.

6 Squeeze out all the excess water from spinach and fenugreek leaves. Add to the masala. Cook on high flame till all the excess water evaporates.

7 Now add the washed chicken pieces and bhuno or stir fry on medium flame stirring constantly, for about 10 minutes. Cook till water evaporates and the masala sticks to the chicken pieces.

8 Add milk or water. Reduce heat. Cover and cook for 8-10 minutes till chicken is tender.

9 Remove cover and again cook for 2 to 3 minutes or till chicken pieces are coated with spinach masala.

10 Garnish with cream. Serve hot.

Kashmiri Chicken Kalia

Serves 6-7

1 chicken (1 kg) - cut into 12 pieces
5 tbsp oil, 5-6 cloves (*laung*), 2" cinnamon (*dalchini*)
2 bay leaves (*tej patta*), 1 onion - ground to a paste, ½ tsp asafoetida (*hing*)
¾ tsp turmeric powder (*haldi*), 1 cup yogurt - well beaten
2½ tsp fennel (*saunf*) powder
1½ tsp dry ginger powder (*sonth*), 1 tsp salt, ½ tsp garam masala
seeds of 2 black and 5-6 green cardamoms (*elaichi*) - coarsely ground
a pinch of saffron (*kesar*) - dissolved in 1 tbsp warm water

1   Heat oil. Add cloves, cinnamon and bay leaves. Fry for a minute till fragrant.

2   Add onion paste. Stir till transparent. Do not let it turn brown.

3   Add asafoetida and turmeric powder. Fry for 1 minute.

4   Add chicken. Fry for 3-4 minutes. Mix together beaten yogurt, fennel, dry ginger powder, salt & ¼ cup water. Mix well.

5   Reduce heat. Pour the yogurt mixture over the chicken. Stir for 2-3 minutes.

6   Add crushed black and green cardamom powder.

7   Add 1 cup water, cover and cook on low heat till chicken is well cooked.

8   Add saffron and garam masala. Simmer for a few minutes and serve hot.

Murg Kaali Mirch

Serves 4

1 chicken - cut into 8 or 12 pieces, 6 tbsp oil
2 tbsp butter, 2 onions - finely sliced, 2 onions - ground to a paste
1 tsp ginger paste, 1 tsp garlic paste, 1 tsp salt, or to taste
2 tsp freshly ground peppercorns, ¼ tsp *haldi* powder, 2 tbsp vinegar

1   Mix ginger, garlic, salt, pepper, turmeric and vinegar with the chicken. Marinate for at least 2-3 hours or longer in the refrigerator.

2   Heat oil and butter in a kadhai and fry the sliced onions till light golden. Add the ground onion paste & fry till golden brown.

3   Add the marinated chicken and stir fry for 5 minutes. Add about ¾ cup water and cook covered on medium fire for about 10 minutes till chicken turns soft. Uncover the pan and cook till dry and the oil comes on top. Sprinkle some freshly crushed peppercorns and serve hot.

Murg Methi

Serves 4-6

1 kg chicken, cut into 12 pieces
4 cups fresh fenugreek leaves (*methi*)
4 medium onions - cut each into half and the cut each half into thin
slices widthwise to get half rings
¼ cup oil
4-6 green chillies - chopped
1 tsp ginger paste, 2 tsp garlic paste
1 tsp red chilli powder, 1½ tsp salt or to taste, ½ tsp turmeric powder
3-4 medium size (250 gm) tomatoes - very finely chopped

1. Heat oil in a heavy, wide-based kadhai. Add onions and cook for 8-10 minutes till golden brown. Add chillies, ginger, garlic and turmeric and fry for a minute.

2. Add chicken and fenugreek leaves and stir fry for about 5 minutes till the chicken turns whitish from all sides and the water somewhat dries up.

3. Add tomatoes, salt, red chilli powder and cook for 5-7 minutes on medium flame till the oil separates. Add about ¾ cup water. Cook covered on low-medium heat for 5-7 minutes till the chicken is tender, leaving just a little gravy to coat chicken.

Kadhai Murg

Serves 4-6

1 medium sized (800 gm) chicken - cut into 12 pieces, 6-7 tbsp oil
1 tbsp coriander (*dhania*) seeds, 3 whole, dry red chillies
½ tsp fenugreek (*methi*) seeds, 3 large onions - cut into slices
15-20 flakes garlic - crushed & chopped
1" pieces of ginger - crushed to a paste (1 tbsp)
4 large tomatoes - chopped
½ cup ready-made tomato puree or ¾ cup homemade puree
1 tsp red chilli powder, 1 tsp ground coriander powder
2 tsp salt, or to taste, ¼ tsp dry mango powder (*amchoor*)
½ tsp garam masala, ½ cup chopped green coriander
1 capsicum - cut into slices, 1" piece ginger - cut into match sticks
1-2 green chillies - cut into long slices
½ cup cream, optional

1. Put coriander seeds and whole red chillies on a *tawa*. Keep on fire and roast lightly till it just starts to change colour. Do not make them brown. Remove from fire.

2. Crush the coriander seeds on a rolling board and pin (*chakla-belan*) to split the seeds. Keep red chillies whole. Keep aside.

3. Heat oil in a kadhai. Reduce heat. Add fenugreek seeds and whole red chillies and stir for a few seconds till fenugreek seeds turns golden.

4. Add onion and cook on medium heat till light brown.

5. Add garlic and stir for 1 minute. Add ginger paste.

6. Add the coriander seeds, red chilli powder and coriander powder.

7. Add chicken and bhuno for 10 minutes on medium flame, stirring well so that chicken attains a nice golden colour.

8. Add chopped tomatoes. Add salt, dry mango powder and garam masala. Stir till dry. Cover and cook for 5-7 minutes or till tender, stirring occasionally.

9. Add tomato puree and chopped green coriander. Cook for 5 minutes.

10. Add the capsicum, ginger match sticks and green chilli slices. Mix well.

11. Reduce heat. Add cream. Mix well for 2-3 minutes and remove from fire. Serve hot.

Hyderabadi Korma Masala

Serves 4

½ kg boneless chicken- cut into 1" pieces

2 medium onions - finely sliced

1 tsp salt or to taste, ¼ tsp turmeric powder, 1 tsp red chilli powder

1¾ cups yogurt (*dahi*) - well beaten

2 tbsp melon seeds (*magaz*) or cashews (*kaju*) - ground in a small mixer without water, ¼ cup chopped coriander

ONION PASTE

2 medium sized onions, ¼" piece of ginger, 2-3 flakes of garlic

1   Grind all ingredients of onion paste to a smooth paste.

2   Heat 5 tbsp oil, add sliced onions and fry till golden.

3   Add the onion paste. Fry till onions turn golden brown.

4   Add chicken and bhuno (fry) for 7- 8 minutes. Keep scraping the sides of the kadhai if masala sticks to the sides or bottom of the kadhai. Add 2 tbsp water in between, mix well. Continue to bhuno, stirring so that the masala doesn't stick to the kadhai.

5   Add salt, turmeric and red chilli powder.

6   Reduce heat, add well beaten yogurt, stirring continuously with the other hand.

7   Add ground magaz or cashews and coriander. Mix well.

8   Add ¼ cup water, mix and cook covered on slow fire, stirring once in between. Cook till the chicken gets tender for about 5-6 minutes and the oil separates. Serve with nan or parantha.

Sirka Pyaz Murg

Serves 8-10

1 kg boneless chicken, 6 onions - chopped
1 cup vinegar (preferably use brown, white can also be used)
1½ tsp black cumin (*shah jeera*)
seeds of 5 green cardamoms (*chhoti elaichi*)- crushed, 8 cloves - crushed
8 flakes garlic - chopped, 1" piece ginger - shredded
4 tomatoes - chopped, 2 green chillies - chopped
½ cup chopped mint leaves (*poodina*)
¼ cup chopped coriander, 1¾ tsp salt or to taste, 1 tsp garam masala
½ tsp red chilli powder, ½ tsp turmeric powder (*haldi*)
a big pinch of red colour (optional), 4 tbsp thick cream

1. Wash chicken and pat dry with a towel. Cut into 1" pieces. Sprinkle some salt, red chilli powder and 1 tbsp ginger-garlic paste. Keep aside for 30 minutes.

2. Chop onions finely. Boil onions & vinegar together in a pan for 4-5 minutes. Drain through a sieve (*channi*) and reserve the vinegar. Keep aside.

3. Heat 7 tbsp oil in a non-stick pan, add black cumin, green cardamoms and cloves. Stir fry for a minute.

4. Add garlic, ginger and boiled chopped onions, and fry for 3-4 minutes on medium flame.

5. Add chicken and cook on medium flame for 7-8 minutes, stirring frequently.

6. Add chopped tomatoes, salt, garam masala, red chilli powder and turmeric powder. Cook for 7-8 minutes on medium heat or till oil separates.

7. Add green chillies, mint, coriander and colour. Cook for 1 minute.

8. Add some strained vinegar from the onions. Mix well. Add ½ cup water and bring to a boil. Simmer for 2-3 minutes and check for tenderness. Add cream, mix well. Remove from fire, serve hot.

Goan Chicken Curry

Serves 4

400 gms boneless chicken - cut into 1" pieces, juice of 1 lemon
½ tsp salt and ½ tsp pepper

GRIND TO A PASTE
½ cup + 2 tbsp fresh coconut - grated
10 dry, red chillies
1 tsp cumin seeds (*jeera*)
1 tbsp coriander seeds (*saboot dhania*)
a pinch of turmeric powder (*haldi*)
1 tbsp tamarind (*imli*) - deseeded
1" piece ginger, 5-6 flakes garlic

OTHER INGREDIENTS
4-5 tbsp oil, 1 onion - chopped
2 tomatoes - chopped
1 cup coconut milk or 1 packet (6 tbsp) coconut milk powder (maggi)
mixed with 1 cup milk and 1 cup water
¾ tsp salt or to taste

BATTER
½ cup gramflour (*besan*), 3 tbsp chopped coriander
½ tsp each of salt, garam masala, pepper & turmeric

1   Marinate chicken with lemon juice, salt and pepper for 15 minutes.

2   Grind coconut, dry red chillies, cumin seeds, coriander seeds, turmeric, tamarind, ginger, garlic and ½ cup water to a paste. Keep coconut paste aside.

3   Heat 4-5 tbsp oil in a kadhai. Add chopped onions & saute till golden brown.

4   Add the tomatoes and cook for 5-6 minutes or till oil separates.

5   Add the prepared ground coconut paste, cook on slow fire for 8-10 minutes.

6   Add coconut milk. Boil, stirring in between. Add salt to taste. Remove from fire.

7   Mix all the ingredients given under batter with ¼ cup water to get a thick batter. Dip the chicken pieces in this batter and deep fry in hot oil to a golden colour.

8   At the time of serving, add the fried chicken to the gravy and heat thoroughly. Serve hot.

Chicken Degi

Serves 4

500 gms boneless chicken - cut into 6 pieces

1 tbsp poppy seeds (*khus-khus*) & 2 tbsp magaz or 3 tbsp cashew (*kaju*)

1 tomato, 4 onions - sliced finely

2 tbsp dry fenugreek leaves (*kasoori methi*)

¼ cup fresh yogurt - well beaten till smooth

4 tbsp and 2 tbsp oil (6 tbsp), ½ tsp chopped coriander

1½ tsp salt, or to taste, ½ tsp pepper, ½ tsp degi lal mirch

¾ tsp garam masala, seeds of 2 black cardamom (*moti illaichi*) - crushed

2 cups water, ½ cup milk

1. Soak poppy seeds and magaz in ¼ cup water for 15 minutes.

2. Boil 1 cup of water and add tomato. Cook covered for 2-3 minutes. Remove from water and peel the skin. Grind to a puree.

3. Heat 4 tbsp oil and fry onions till they turn golden brown. Remove from fire. Cool.

4. Grind soaked magaz, poppy seeds and fried onions to a brown paste in the mixer-grinder.

5. Heat 2 tbsp oil. Add the onion paste and cook on low heat for 3-5 minutes.

6. Add beaten yogurt & cook for 3-4 minutes or till the paste turns brown again.

7. Add the chicken and stir fry for 8-10 minutes.

8. Add the prepared blanched, pureed tomato. Add salt, pepper, degi mirch, garam masala and crushed black cardamoms. Cook for 3- 4 minutes or till oil separates. Add coriander.

9. Add 2 cups water, give 1-2 boils. Simmer for 6-7 minutes.

10. Remove from fire, add milk, stirring continuously. Return to very low heat, cook on low flame for 1-2 minutes. Serve hot.

Continental

Chicken Mince Lasagne

Serves 7-8

8 lasagne sheets, ready made
1 cup grated cheese, preferably mozzarella

FILLING
½ kg minced chicken (*keema*), 1 tsp salt, ½ tsp pepper
2½ cups ready made tomato puree, ½ tsp orgeano

CHEESE SAUCE
3 tbsp butter, 4 tbsp flour (*maida*), 3 cups milk
½ cup grated cheese (preferably use mozzarella)
½ tsp salt, ¼ tsp freshly ground pepper, ½ tsp orgeano

1. Heat 4 tbsp oil in a pressure cooker, add mince and cook for 2-3 minutes.

2. Add salt, pepper, ready-made tomato puree, orgeano and ½ cup of water. Pressure cook to give 2 whistles. Let the pressure drop by itself. Keep filling aside.

3. For lasagne sheets, in a shallow pan or a kadhai boil water with some salt, slip one lasagne sheet at a time to prevent them from sticking together. When one is half done, slip the second one. Do not boil too many sheets at a time.

4. Simmer gently for about 5 minutes or until they are no longer stiff and can bend.

5. Cover a tray with aluminium foil. Grease it. Remove sheets from water and spread out on the tray in one single layer, without overlapping. Cover with a cloth and keep aside.

6. To make the sauce melt butter, add the flour and stir for 1 minute on low heat. Add the milk, stirring continuously. Stir until the sauce comes to a boil. Remove from fire. Add cheese, salt, orgeano and pepper.

7. To assemble the lasagne, grease a rectangle or square baking dish with some butter or oil. Spread 2-3 tbsp sauce at the bottom of the dish. Put a layer of boiled lasagne sheet in the dish.

8. Pour a little cheese sauce (about 2 tbsp) on the lasagne sheet.

9. Spread 2 heaped tbsp of the chicken mixture over the sauce. Sprinkle some cheese. Continue layers this way until all the mixture is used. End with a thick layer of sauce. Sprinkle ½ cup grated cheese.

10. Cover dish loosely with aluminium foil and bake in a hot oven at 180°C/ 350°F for 25 minutes. Uncover and bake for another 10 minutes. Serve hot.

Pasta Arabiata

Serves 4

250 gm boneless chicken (2 chicken breasts) - cut into ½" pieces

2 cups macaroni or penne pasta or any other shape

3 tbsp olive oil, 2 tbsp butter, 1 tsp garlic crushed

2 dry red chillies - cut into diagonal slices with a pair of scissors

1 onion - very finely chopped, 2 tbsp chopped celery, 500 gm tomatoes

¼ cup ready made tomato puree, 1 tbsp tomato ketchup

½ cup pasta water or stock, ½ capsicum - chopped very finely

1 tsp flour (*maida*), 1¼ tsp salt, ½ tsp pepper, 1 tsp oregano

1 tsp red chilli flakes

1. Boil 8 cups water. Add tomatoes. Boil for 3-4 minutes. Remove tomatoes from water with a slotted spoon. Keep aside to cool. Peel tomatoes. Chop tomatoes roughly, churn them in a mixer for a few seconds to a rough puree. Keep aside.

2. To the boiling water, add 1 tsp salt and 1 tbsp oil. Add pasta to boiling water. Stir to see that pasta is not sticking to the bottom of the pan. Boil, stirring occasionally, for about 7-8 minutes till pasta turns almost soft, but yet firm. Remove from fire and leave pasta in hot water for 2-3 minutes. Strain, reserving 1½ cups of pasta water. Spoon 1 tbsp olive oil on the pasta. Cover and keep aside.

3. Heat 3 tbsp olive oil in a pan. Add garlic, onion and celery. Cook for about 2-3 minutes, till onions turn soft. Add ½ tsp salt. Add chicken, stir fry for 2-3 minutes till it turns whitish. Sprinkle a little water. Cook covered for 1 minute till soft. Remove from pan. Keep aside.

4. Melt 2 tbsp butter in the same pan. Add red chillies. Stir till they start to darken. Add pureed tomatoes. Cook for 4-5 minutes or till almost dry and leave fat. Add tomato puree and ketchup. Stir for 2 minutes. Add capsicum and flour. Mix well for ½ minute. Add salt, pepper, oregano, chilli flakes & 1 cup pasta water. Boil for a minute. Add chicken and pasta. Mix well. Remove from fire. Check seasonings.

5. To serve, heat pasta. Add some pasta water if needed to loosen the sauce, but do not make it runny. The sauce should just coat the pasta. Serve hot with bread.

Tip:
- Pasta is cooked to the "al dente" stage - tender but firm to bite. To test, press a piece against the side of the pan with a fork. It should need a firm pressure to break the pasta.

Chicken Stroganoff

Serves 4

2 boneless chicken thigh or breast - cut into ½" cubes (200 gm)

½ tsp salt, ¼ tsp pepper and a pinch red chilli powder

1 chicken soup cube , 2 tbsp butter and 1 tbsp oil

1 small onion - finely chopped

1 tbsp chopped celery

100 gms (8-10) mushrooms - each cut into 2 pieces

3-4 flakes garlic - crushed, 1 tbsp flour

½ tbsp tomato puree, 1 tbsp tomato ketchup

½ tsp worcestershire or HP sauce, ¾ cup cream

1½ tbsp cheese spread

1 tsp mustard sauce

1. Crush soup cube and mix with 1½ cups water. Bring to a boil and let it simmer for 2-3 minutes to make stock. Keep stock aside.

2. Sprinkle some salt, pepper and pinch of chilli powder over the chicken pieces. Mix well.

3. Heat 1 tbsp butter in a pan. Add onion and cook till golden. Add celery and stir for 2 minutes till onions turn light brown. Add mushrooms and cook for 3-4 minutes till golden. Remove the vegetables from the pan.

4. In the same pan heat 1 tbsp of butter and 1 tbsp oil together. Add the chicken pieces. Stir till they are well browned on both sides. Add garlic and stir for a few seconds.

5. Add tomato puree, tomato sauce, HP sauce and stir for a few seconds. Add sauted vegetables to the chicken.

6. Take out ½ cup of prepared chicken stock and blend in 1 tbsp flour. Add the remaining stock and the flour paste to the chicken. Bring to a boil. Simmer for 2 minutes till chicken turns tender. Remove from fire.

7. Whisk cream, cheese spread and mustard well so that there are no lumps and it is smooth.

8. Take pan off the heat. Add cream and cheese spread mixture and mix well.

9. Heat on very low flame gently and remove when it starts to boil. Check salt. Serve with rice or bread.

Chicken Moussaka

Serves 8

250 gm chicken mince

3 tbsp olive oil, 1 flake garlic crushe

2 onions - sliced thinly, 2 tomatoes - blanched, peeled and chopped

3 tbsp tomato puree, salt and pepper to taste, ¼ tsp chilli flakes

2 potatoes - cut into thin round slices

6 long brinjals - cut diagonally into long pieces

ALL SPICE POWDER

2 cloves (*laung*), 5 pepper corns (*saboot kali mirch*)

2 blades star anise, 2 pinches nutmeg powder, ½" cinnamon stick (*dalchini*)

BECHAMEL SAUCE

3 tbsp butter, 3 tbsp flour (*maida*), 2 cups milk, 1 cheese cube - grated

1 egg, ¼ tsp each of - nutmeg, white pepper and salt

TOPPING (MIX TOGETHER)

2 tbsp olive oil, ½ tsp mixed herbs or 2 tbsp chopped fresh herbs
(coriander/mint/basil)

1 tsp garlic paste

1. Sprinkle some salt on the brinjal pieces. Keep aside for 10 minutes to sweat. Pat dry and deep fry till light golden. Do not over fry.

2. Boil potato slices in 4 cups water with 1 tsp salt and 1 tsp lemon juice, till soft.

3. Heat olive oil in a pan. Add garlic. When it just starts to change colour, add onion and cook till light brown. Add minced chicken and cook for 3-4 minutes till it changes colour. Add blanched and chopped tomatoes. Saute fro a minute. Add tomato puree and seasonings. Remove from fire.

4. For bechamel sauce, melt butter in a pan. Add flour and stir for a minute. Remove from fire and add milk, stirring continuously till it thickens. Add seasonings. Remove from fire. Let it cool slightly. Add cheese and egg and mix well. Keep aside.

5. To assemble, grease a medium square dish. Put a layer of eggplant. Spread mince on it. Repeat layer of eggplant and mince. Pour the bechamel sauce on it. Finally arrange the potatoes overlapping. Brush with olive oil mixed with herbs and garlic.

6. Bake for 15 minutes at 200°C. Grill for 5 minutes till golden. Serve.

Stuffed Roast Chicken

Serves 4

1 small chicken (broiler) of 700 gm

50 gms butter, 1 tsp thyme, ¾ tsp pepper, 1 tsp paprika, ½ tsp salt

4 flakes garlic - chopped finely, 1 tbsp lemon juice

STUFFING

2 onions - sliced and deep fried

½ cup grated smoked gouda cheese or cheddar cheese

2 cups chopped spinach, 2 tbsp chopped celery or parsley or coriander

2 tbsp olive oil, 1 tsp finely chopped garlic, ½ cup fresh bread cubes

1 tbsp finely chopped pine nuts or almonds, ¼ tsp nutmeg

FOR SAUCE

2 tbsp butter, 1 tsp garlic crushed

1½ tsp flour, 1½ cups water, 1 cube chicken seasoning

2-3 tsp worcestershire or HP sauce, few drops tabasco sauce

¼ tsp pepper, a pinch of brown sugar

GLAZE

2 tbsp butter, 1 tsp honey, 1 tsp lemon juice

1. Wash chicken. Pat dry top & cavity of chicken with paper towels. Make 4 light cuts on it. Mix melted butter with thyme, pepper, paprika, salt, garlic, lemon juice. Rub this over and inside the chicken. Marinate chicken for 1-2 hours.

2. For the filling, microwave washed spinach for 2 minutes till slightly soft. Discard excess water. Squeeze lightly. Add all other ingredients of the stuffing. Mix well. Stuff in the chicken cavity. Close the cavity with wooden skewers or stitch up with a cotton thread.

3. Heat butter till it turns brown. Remove from fire and add honey and lemon juice. Brush glaze on the chicken.

4. Wrap the chicken in foil. Place on a greased roasting tray. Roast in a preheated oven for 20 minutes at 190°C. Then remove foil and bake for 25 minutes, until the chicken is no longer pink when you cut into the thickest part.

5. For sauce, heat 2 tbsp butter in a pan add crushed garlic to it and stir till garlic changes colour. Mix chicken seasoning cube, flour with 1½ cups water and add to the garlic. Stir till it boils. Add tabasco sauce, HP sauce, sugar and pepper to it. Simmer for 5 minutes. Check seasoning.

6. Place roasted chicken in a serving dish. Pour hot sauce over the chicken. Decorate with boiled and sauted potatoes and fresh green herbs.

Chicken Baked with Macaroni

Serves 4-5

250-300 gm boneless chicken - cut into 1" pieces

50 gm macaroni (½ cup)

1 tbsp butter

1 small capsicum - deseeded and chopped

1 small firm tomato - deseeded and chopped

SAUCE

1 small onion - chopped

2 tbsp butter

2½ tbsp flour (*maida*)

1 cup milk

4 tbsp tomato puree

1 tbsp tomato sauce

salt and pepper to taste

2 tbsp chopped parsley or coriander

GARNISH

3-4 almonds - cut into thin long pieces, some grated cheese

1   Heat 1 tbsp butter in a pressure cooker. Add the chicken pieces and stir fry for 2-3 minutes. Add 1½ cups water and pressure cook to give 2 whistles. Remove from heat. Let the pressure drop. Strain and reserve the stock for sauce and keep the chicken pieces aside.

2   Boil 2 cups of water. Add macaroni and boil for 7-8 minutes till tender. Drain and refresh under cold water. Strain and keep aside in the strainer for all the water to drain out.

3   To prepare the sauce, heat butter in a pan and add onions. Stir till they turn soft and slightly change colour. Add the flour and stir till light brown. Mix stock and milk to get 2½ cups. Lower heat and add the stock-milk mixture. Stir till smooth and creamy. Remove from heat. Add tomato puree, tomato sauce, salt, pepper and chopped parsley or coriander.

4   Add macaroni, chicken, capsicum and tomato. Stir well and check the seasoning, adjust according to taste.

5   Pour the mixture in a baking dish. Top with grated cheese and almonds. Bake in a moderate oven at 180°C for 15 minutes. Serve hot with buttered toasts cut into triangles.

Quick Pasta with Chicken & Spinach

Serves 3-4

2 cups pasta, such as fussili or fettuccine
2 skinless chicken breast fillets, cut into thin strips
2 cups spinach leaves, thick stems removed
2 tbsp olive oil, 1 tsp crushed garlic
200 ml (1 cup) cream
3 tbsp fresh basil leaves, roughly chopped
salt and freshly ground black pepper to taste
½ tsp oregano, ¼ tsp lemon juice, lemon wedges, to serve

1 Cook the pasta in a large pan of salted boiling water for 8-10 minutes, until just tender.

2 Add spinach leaves to pasta and keep aside for 2 minutes in water for the leaves to wilt and become soft. Strain after 2 minutes, reserving ½ cup of pasta water. Keep pasta and spinach aside.

3 Heat the oil in a large frying pan, add garlic. Stir and add the chicken and fry over medium heat for 3-4 minutes, stirring often, until cooked.

4 Add the cream, basil and ½ cup of pasta water. Add salt, pepper and oregano to taste.

5 Add the pasta and spinach and mix well. Squeeze a little lemon and serve hot.

Chicken with Olives & Tomatoes

Serves 3-4

200 gm boneless chicken - cut into 1" pieces

12 olives

4 large tomatoes - blanched and skinned

3 tbsp oil or butter

2 flakes garlic - crushed

1 tsp salt

½ tsp pepper

1 tbsp coriander - chopped

1. In a nonstick pan, melt 1 tbsp of butter, add the chicken pieces and fry on medium heat till for 3-4 minutes till they change colour. Add ¼ tsp salt and ¼ tsp pepper.

2. Sprinkle about 2 tbsp water in the chicken and cook covered for 4-5 minutes till the pieces are tender. Drain the left over butter if any, keep aside the chicken pieces.

3. To make the sauce, put tomatoes in hot water for 3-4 minutes. Remove skin and grind them in a liquidizer to a puree.

4. Heat 1 tbsp oil. Add garlic, add the pureed tomatoes. Cook for 5 minutes till slightly thick.

5. Add the olives and ½ tsp salt and ¼ tsp pepper or to taste. Remove from fire. Keep the sauce aside.

6. Spread ¼ of the sauce in a greased serving dish. Arrange the chicken pieces on it and pour the remaining sauce.

7. Sprinkle coriander.

8. Bake in a preheated oven at 180°C/350°F/Gas mark 4 for 10-15 minutes.

Mince Steak with Mushroom Sauce

Serves 2 (Makes 4 steaks)

MINCE STEAKS
300 gm chicken mince (*keema*)
½ onion - chopped very finely, 1 tsp ginger-garlic paste
1 slice bread - grind in a mixer to get fresh crumbs
1 tsp worcestershire sauce, 1 tsp salt & ¼ tsp pepper to taste

FILLING (HERBED CHEESE)
4-5 tbsp grated mozzarella or pizza cheese, ½ tsp dried oregano
1 tbsp finely chopped fresh parsley or coriander

MUSHROOM SAUCE
1 tbsp butter, 3-4 mushrooms - finely chopped, 1½ tbsp flour (*maida*)
1 cup hot water mixed with 1 stock cube (soup cube)
½ tsp worcestershire sauce
2 tbsp tomato puree, 1 tsp tomato sauce, pepper to taste

1. Grind the chicken mince in a mixer for a few seconds to get more binding in the chicken mince. In a bowl, combine chicken mince, onion, ginger-garlic paste, fresh bread crumbs, worcestershire sauce, salt and pepper. Mix well.

2. Mix all ingredients of the filling together. Keep aside.

3. Form 4 balls from the mince mixture. Flatten each ball and put a tbsp of herbed cheese inside. Shape into a ball again and flatten to form 4 steaks. Refrigerate till the time of serving.

4. To prepare the sauce, heat butter and fry the mushrooms until golden brown. Add the flour and fry on low heat until brown. Remove from heat. Add the stock cube mixed in hot water. Add worcestershire sauce, tomato puree and tomato sauce. Return to fire. Boil. Cook stirring continuously for 3-4 minutes till thick. Add pepper to taste. Remove from fire.

5. To serve, heat ½-1 tbsp oil on low heat in a nonstick pan and coat the bottom of the pan with this oil. Add the steaks. Cook steaks on low heat for about 8-10 minutes. Keep turning sides and pressing the steaks occasionally so that the steaks get cooked from inside and also turn brown on both sides.

6. Transfer to a serving platter. Pour hot mushroom sauce over them. Accompany the steaks with boiled vegetables drizzled with olive oil and rice or bread.

Chicken Burritos with Red Sauce

Serves 3-4

6 flour tortillas (thin, big, flour chappatis, available ready made)

RED SAUCE
4-5 Kashmiri dry, red chillies
6 medium sized tomatoes
1½ tsp crushed garlic, ¾ tsp salt, ¾ tsp red chilli powder
¾ cup water mixed with 1 soup cube (maggi)
¾ tsp dried basil or thyme (optional)
¾ tsp dried oregano
3½ tbsp tomato sauce
a big pinch of orange red colour (optional)

FILLING
400 gm boneless chicken - cut into ½" pieces
6 tbsp butter, 2 tsp garlic chopped
2 tbsp plain flour (*maida*)
1½ cups milk, ½ tsp salt
6 tbsp grated cheddar cheese (tin or cubes)
1½ cups boiled (cooked) rice
2 tbsp chopped pickled jalapenos or 2-3 green chillies - finely chopped
6 tbsp chopped fresh coriander

1   Roast the chillies on a pan. Roast tomatoes by piercing them with a fork and holding over a naked gas flame. Roast until black patches appear on them. Do not peel the tomatoes, chop with the peel.

2   Place the roasted chillies, tomatoes and all other ingredients written under red sauce including water mixed with soup cube in a mixer. Churn or grind well to a fine puree.

3   Heat 1 tbsp butter or oil in a pan. Add the prepared sauce, give one boil. Cook for 3-4 minutes till it becomes slightly thick. Remove from fire, keep sauce aside.

4   For the filling, heat butter. Add garlic. Stir fry for 30 seconds.

5   Add chicken and stir for 2-3 minutes till the pieces get lightly browned from various sides and get cooked.

6   Reduce heat. Add flour. Mix and fry for 1 minute.

7   Add milk and cook stirring till the sauce just starts to get thick. Remove from fire. Add 3 tbsp cheese.

8   Add boiled rice, chopped jalapenos and coriander. Mix gently so that the rice grains do not break. Check for salt. Keep aside.

9   To assemble, place 3-4 tbsp of filling on a tortilla, a little away from one end. Fold over and roll froward to get a roll. Repeat with the remaining filling and tortillas.

10 To serve, warm the rolls in a microwave or shallow fry 2 rolls at a time till golden in a pan with 2 tbsp of oil with the tucked side down first in oil. Change side using 2 spoons and cook till golden brown from all the sides.

11 Pour some heated red chilli sauce on the burritos and serve garnished with the remaining 3 tbsp cheese.

Chicken Sizzler

Serves 4

MARINATE TOGETHER

2 small chicken breasts, 3 tbsp olive oil, 1 tsp salt, 1 tsp pepper

1 tbsp garlic paste, 2 tsp mustard paste, 2½ tbsp balsamic vinegar

FILLING

4-5 tbsp grated mozzarella, ½ tsp oregano

1 tbsp finely chopped basil or coriander

GINGER ORANGE SAUCE

2 tbsp olive oil, 1 tsp lemon rind, ¼ tsp salt, ¼ tsp pepper

1 tbsp shredded basil

4 tbsp orange tang & 3 tbsp cornflour dissolved in ¼ cup water

½ tbsp lemon juice, 1 tsp ginger juice (finely grate 1 tbsp ginger & squeeze)

TO SERVE

2 cabbage leaves - torn into pieces, a few french fries

3 cups boiled rice mixed with ½ tsp oregano, ½ tsp red chilli flakes

salt to taste and 2 tbsp finely chopped coriander to make coriander rice

1. Wash and pat dry chicken. Slit into half widthwise, keeping one side joint so that the breast opens up like a butterfly. Prick lightly. Mix all ingredients of the marinade. Add chicken to it and rub well to coat the chicken. Keep aside for at least 2-3 hours in the fridge.

2. Put marinated chicken in a pressure cooker with 1 cup water. Allow 2 whistles. Remove from heat and let the pressure drop by itself. When it cools, keep breast aside and use the stock (liquid) for the sauce.

3. For the sauce, heat olive oil. Add the above stock. Bring to a boil. Add orange tang and cornflour dissolved in water, stirring constantly. Cook for a minute only. Remove from fire. Add orange or lemon rind, ginger juice, lemon juice and basil. Add salt pepper if needed.

4. To serve, heat a pan with 1 tbsp oil. Open out the marinated chicken breast and place on the pan. Cook on medium heat, pressing occasionally, for about 1 minute on each side till the chicken is golden. Remove from pan. Sprinkle some cheese, oregano and basil on one side of the hot breast and turn over to cover to make a complete breast.

5. Sprinkle a mixture of 1 tbsp oil and 1 tbsp water on the wooden plate. Keep aside. Heat the iron sizzler plate on high flame. Place a few cabbage leaves on the iron plate. Spread rice on it. Arrange vegetables and french fries on the sides. Place a piece of chicken in the centre. Spoon sauce on the chicken and let it fall on the plate. Place iron plate on the wooden plate to sizzle and make fumes. Serve.

Stuffed Chicken with Sauce

Serves 4

4 chicken breasts with just 1 wing bone or 4 chicken breasts - boneless
3 tbsp olive oil, ½ tsp pepper, ½ tsp salt

FILLING
½ cup grated cheddar cheese (tin or cubes), ¼ tsp salt, ¼ tsp oregano
½ tsp pepper, or to taste, ½ tbsp butter, 1 tbsp chopped coriander
4 black or green olives - chopped (optional)

SAFFRON SAUCE
1 tbsp butter, 1 cup milk, ½ cup cream, 4 tbsp cheese spread
½ tsp salt and ½ tsp white pepper or to taste,
1 tbsp cornflour dissolved in ½ cup water
1 tbsp chopped chives or parsley or coriander
½ tsp saffron (*kesar*) dissolved in 2 tbsp warm water for 15 minutes

1   Make a slit in chicken breast lengthwise (at the open end) almost till the end keeping the end intact. Open up the breast to get a big heart shaped piece. If using chicken with bone, after making the slit do not open up the slit as done for boneless, but just push inside the slit with the fingers, forming a pocket.

2   Mix 3 tbsp olive oil, ½ tsp pepper and salt in a big flat plate. Roll the chicken breast over the marinade on both the sides. Keep aside for 2-3 hours.

3   For the filling, mix all the ingredients well. Divide the filling into 4 portions.

4   Take a marinated breast with bone, keep it on a flat surface. Spread 1 portion of filling inside the slit of the breast, spread on all sides completely with your fingers. For boneless breast spread 1 portion of filling on one piece, spreading on all sides completely. Pick up the other side & fold it forward over the filling. Repeat with the remaining breasts. Keep aside for atleast ½ hour in the fridge.

5   Heat an oven to 160°C. Place chicken breast in the oven, on a wire rack covered with foil and greased. Bake for 15 minutes. Pour some oil and change sides carefully and bake for another 15 minutes or till done.

6   For the sauce, mix all the ingredients of the sauce with a whisk. Keep on low heat. Bring to a boil, stirring on low heat and then simmer for 2-3 seconds. Remove from fire.

7   To serve, spread the sauce in the plate, and place one grilled chicken breast on the sauce. Pour some more sauce on the breast. Serve immediately with some boiled and sauteed vegetables.

Chicken & Mushroom Augratin

Serves 4-6

300 chicken
3 tbsp butter
2 onions - chopped, 200 gm mushrooms - each cut into 4 pieces
3 tbsp plain flour (*maida*), 3 cups milk
salt, pepper to taste, 3 cubes (60 gm) cheese - grated
4 tbsp dry bread crumbs, ½ tsp red chilli flakes (optional)

1   Put chicken in a pressure cooker with ½ tsp salt and pepper. Allow 2 whistles. After it cools, shred the chicken into pieces. Discard bones.

2   Cut each mushroom into 4 pieces.

3   Melt butter in a heavy bottomed pan. Add onions and cook till transparent.

4   Add mushrooms. Stir for 2 minutes.

5   Sprinkle flour. Stir continuously for a minute on low heat. Remove from fire.

6   Add the milk, stirring continuously. Return to fire. Cook, stirring continuously till it coats the back of the spoon. Add salt and pepper to taste. Remove from heat.

7   Add boiled chicken and mix well. Add grated cheese.

8   Transfer to a baking dish.

9   Mix bread crumbs and red chilli flakes. Sprinkle on the dish. Keep aside till serving time.

10 Grill in a preheated oven for about 10 minutes till the dish gets browned. Serve hot with buttered toasts.

Italian Chicken Cacciatore

Serves 3-4

3 chicken breasts (400 gm) or 4 legs , 3-4 tbsp oil, preferably olive oil
2 tsp finely chopped garlic, 1 large onion - chopped finely (1 cup)
½ cup ready made tomato puree, 2 large tomatoes
¼ cup white wine or water
1 tsp vinegar, preferably balsamic vinegar, or to taste
1 bay leaf , 1 tsp dried oregano, 1 tsp dried or fresh thyme (optional)
1 tsp sugar, 1 tsp salt, or to taste, ¾ tsp pepper, 4-6 black olives - halved
1 tbsp chopped dried or fresh parsley, 1 -2 tbsp parmesan cheese

1. To blanch tomatoes - put whole tomatoes in 1 cup boiling water. Cook covered for 5 minutes. Remove tomatoes, and cool them. Churn blanched tomatoes in a mixer to get fresh tomato puree. Strain puree.

2. Pressure cook chicken pieces with ½ cup water & ½ tsp salt to give 2 whistles. Remove from fire and let the pressure drop by itself. Check that chicken is soft. Drain and reserve the stock.

3. Heat 2 tbsp oil in a non stick pan. Add chicken pieces and cook on moderate heat till it is nicely browned. Remove from fire and keep aside.

4. To the same oil, add 1 tbsp more oil and chopped garlic. Fry till it starts to change colour. Add chopped onion and cook till soft, but not browned.

5. Add fresh and ready made tomato puree, wine, vinegar, bay leaf, oregano, thyme, sugar, salt and pepper. Add chicken and stir for 2-3 minutes to mix well.

6. Add the stock. Boil. Lower heat and simmer for 2 minutes till the sauce becomes thick. Add olives and chopped parsley. Serve with boiled pasta tossed in 1 tbsp butter and some freshly crushed peppercorns or dill flakes.

Variation:
Button mushrooms can be added to this dish at step 5 to give it a different flavour.

Chinese and Thai

Chicken in Hot Garlic Sauce

Serves 4

200 gm boneless chicken - cut into ¾" cubes

1 tsp salt, ¼ tsp pepper, 1 tbsp garlic - crushed

2 tbsp cornflour, 2 tbsp plain flour (*maida*), 1 egg

SAUCE

2 tbsp oil, 2 tbsp very finely chopped garlic

2 spring onions (only white part) - cut into thick diagonals

½ onion - cut into triangles, ½ capsicum - cut into triangles

1½ cups chicken stock, see note

1 tsp salt, ¼ tsp ajinomoto, ½ tsp sugar, 1 tbsp red chilli paste

1 tbsp vinegar, 2 tsp soya sauce, 1½ tbsp ketchup

3 tbsp cornflour dissolved in ½ cup water

1. Mix cornflour and plain flour in a bowl. Add egg and mix very well to break all lumps. Add salt, pepper and garlic.

2. Wash and pat dry chicken. Add chicken to the egg mixture.

3. Heat oil for deep frying in a kadhai. Reduce heat. Add all chicken pieces and then increase heat. Fry for only 2-3 minutes till they turn very light golden. Do not fry longer as it will turn the chicken hard. Keep aside.

4. Heat the wok with 2 tbsp oil. Reduce heat and add garlic. Stir 1-2 times.

5. Add chilli paste. Stir. Add both the onions and capsicum and stir fry for 5-10 seconds.

6. Add salt, ajinomoto, sugar, vinegar, soya sauce, ketchup and mix well.

7. Add chicken and stir for 1-2 minutes. Add stock. Increase heat. Let the stock come to a boil.

8. Add the cornflour paste. Stir and let it come to a boil. Simmer for 1-2 minutes till thick. Serve hot with rice or noodles.

Note:

Use 1 chicken stock cube mixed with 1½ cups water if fresh stock is not there. Reduce salt to ½ tsp.

Crispy Honey Chicken

Serves 3-4

2 chicken breasts (300 gm) - keep in the freezer for 1 hour to become firm

½ cup cornflour

BATTER

2 egg-whites, 1 tbsp oil, 1 tbsp cornflour, ½ tsp salt, ½ tsp white pepper

COATING SAUCE

2 tbsp oil, 2-3 dry red chillies - cut diagonally into 1" pieces

4 tbsp tomato ketchup, 2 tbsp honey, ¼ tsp salt, ¼ tsp white pepper

1 tbsp cornflour dissolved in ¼ cup water or stock

2 tsp sesame seeds - toasted on a *tawa* for 2 minutes till light golden

1. Cut the chilled chicken into very thin slices with a serrated knife.

2. Mix all ingredients of the batter well. Add chicken. Keep aside for 1 hour.

3. Pick up the chicken pieces, shaking off the excess marinade and place on a plate. Again pick up the chicken and place on a clean dry plate so that any extra marinade is drained off.

4. Sprinkle ¼ cup cornflour and mix well so as to coat each piece with cornflour. Sprinkle the remaining ¼ cup cornflour and mix again to coat well.

5. Heat oil for frying. Deep fry chicken in 2 batches till light golden and crispy. When adding chicken to oil for frying, keep them spaced out & let each batch be in oil on low medium heat for about 4 minutes. Do not over fry to make the coating brown & too crisp as this may ruin the chicken, making it hard & chewy.

6. Add 2 tbsp oil in a wok or kadhai. Put red chillies. Stir for ½ minute. Remove from fire. Add tomato ketchup, honey, salt, pepper. Mix well. Add cornflour paste. Stir for a minute. Add the chicken and sesame seeds and toss well to coat each piece of chicken evenly. Serve hot.

Chicken Manchurian

Serves 4

250 gm boneless chicken - cut into ¾" pieces

1-2 spring onion - chopped, keep white and greens separate

EGG BATTER

1 egg, 1½ tbsp cornflour

1½ tbsp flour

½ tsp vinegar

1 tsp soya sauce

1 tsp red chilli sauce, ¾ tsp salt & ½ tsp pepper

MANCHURIAN SAUCE

2 tbsp oil

2 tbsp crushed ginger, 2 tbsp crushed garlic

1 green chilli - finely chopped

2 cups chicken stock

1½ tbsp cornflour - dissolved in 3 tbsp water

1 tsp sherry or white wine - optional

1½ tbsp soya sauce

1 tbsp tomato ketchup, 1 tbsp chilli sauce

1 tsp vinegar, ½ tsp salt, ½ tsp pepper, ¼ tsp sugar

¼ tsp ajinomoto, optional

1. Mix all ingredients of the batter. Dip the chicken pieces in egg batter.

2. Heat oil for deep frying in a kadhai. Reduce heat. Add all chicken pieces to the oil and then increase heat. Fry for only 2-3 minutes till they turn very light golden. Do not fry longer as it will turn the chicken hard. Keep aside.

3. In a wok heat oil. Lightly fry garlic and ginger.

4. Add green chillies and white of spring onions. Stir for a few seconds.

5. Reduce heat add chicken stock. Add all other ingredients of the sauce except cornflour. Cook for 2-3 minutes.

6. Add cornflour paste and give one boil. Add fried chicken and cook for 1-2 minutes till sauce turns slightly thick. Serve hot garnished with onion greens.

Chicken in Black Pepper Sauce

Serves 4

200 gm chicken (boneless) - cut into 1" pieces

greens of 1 spring onion - cut into ½" pieces

SAUCE

2 tbsp oil, ½ tsp peppercorns (*saboot kali mirch*)

½ tsp chopped garlic, ½ tsp ginger paste

1 tsp freshly ground black pepper, ½-1 tsp soya sauce, pinch of ajinomoto

1½ tbsp cornflour, 1 tsp vinegar

1½ cups water mixed with 1 chicken soup cube OR 1½ cups stock

MARINADE

1 egg, ½ tsp salt, ¼ tsp ajinomoto, 2 tbsp cornflour, 2 tbsp flour (*maida*)

1   Marinate the chicken in all the ingredients of the marinade and keep aside for at least ½ hour.

2   Heat oil in a wok or a *kadhai* and deep fry the chicken for 2-3 minutes on medium heat or till chicken is soft. Drain and keep aside.

3   For the sauce, heat 2 tbsp oil. Reduce heat add ginger, garlic and peppercorns. Cook till garlic changes colour. Add black pepper, soya sauce, ajinomoto, vinegar and chicken. Stir to mix well.

4   Add water mixed with cube or chicken stock. Boil. Add enough water (½ cup approx.) mixed with cornflour. Cook stirring till it turns to a thick saucy consistency. Add salt to taste. Add vinegar and greens of spring onion. Remove from fire. Serve hot.

Spicy Honey Chicken

Serves 4

250 gm boneless chicken - cut into 1½" pieces
½ cup cornflour - approx., 2-3 dry, red chillies - broken into bits
2 tsp garlic paste or 6- 8 flakes of garlic crushed to a paste
2 tbsp spring onions, 2½ tbsp tomato ketchup, 1½-2 tsp soya sauce
2 tsp honey, 2 tbsp stir fry sauce, oil for frying

MARINADE
2 eggs, ½ tsp salt, ½ tsp ajinomoto (optional), 1 tbsp cornflour, 1 tbsp oil

1 Cut the boneless chicken into 1½" pieces.

2 Mix all the ingredients of the marinade - eggs, salt, ajinomoto, cornflour and oil. Marinate the chicken and keep aside for 1 hour.

3 Chop white part of spring onion finely and cut green portion cut into 1" pieces.

4 Spread about ½ cup cornflour in a flat plate.

5 Pick up each piece of chicken from the marinade and coat with cornflour on all the sides. See to it that each piece is coated well from all sides.

6 Deep fry the chicken for 3-4 minutes till crisp and golden brown. Drain and keep aside.

7 Heat 2 tbsp oil in a wok/kadhai. Reduce heat. Add dry, red chillies and stir. Add garlic paste. Stir for a few seconds.

8 Add finely chopped white part of spring onions, tomato ketchup, soya sauce and honey. Saute for a few seconds.

9 Add the crispy fried chicken and sprinkle the stir fry sauce on it. Stir-fry ensuring that each piece is coated with the sauce. Mix in the greens of spring onions. Serve hot.

Mongolian Chicken

Serves 4

200 gm chicken - cut into bite size (1") pieces
1 tsp red chilli paste, 10 flakes garlic - crushed
2 spring onions - white part finely chopped & greens - cut into 1" pieces
1 cup water mixed with 1 chicken seasoning cube or 1 cup chicken stock
1 tsp soya sauce, 3 tbsp tomato ketchup, ½-1 tbsp vinegar
½ tsp ajinomoto, ½ tsp sugar, 2 tbsp cornflour

MARINADE
1 egg white, ½ tsp salt, ½ tsp pepper, ¼ tsp ajinomoto (optional)
3 tbsp cornflour, 1 tbsp oil, a pinch orange colour, a pinch baking powder

1   Cut chicken into 1" pieces. Marinate the chicken with all the ingredients of the marinade and keep aside for atleast ½ hour.

2   Heat oil in a wok or a kadhai and deep fry the chicken for 2-3 minutes on medium heat till cooked. Remove from oil and keep on a kitchen towel.

3   Heat 2 tbsp more oil, reduce heat and add crushed garlic. Stir and add chilli paste.

4   Add white of spring onions and fry for a minute.

5   Add soya sauce, tomato ketchup, ajinomoto and sugar. Add ½ cup water mixed with seasoning cube or chicken stock. Boil for a minute. Add salt to taste.

6   Dissolve cornflour in ½ cup stock and add to the stock, stirring continuously till the sauce thickens.

7   Add the chicken, green part of spring onions & cook for 1 minute. Add vinegar to taste and remove from fire. Serve hot.

Thai Green Curry with Aubergine

Serves 4

350 gms chicken - boneless or with bones - cut into 1" pieces

150 gms small aubergines (*baingan*) - peeled and cut into ¼" thick slices, see note

green curry paste (given below)

2 cups ready-made coconut milk

1 tsp salt, 1 tsp brown sugar/gur, 10-12 basil leaves chopped

2 tbsp fish sauce, 2-3 lemon leaves

2-3 green/red chillies - slit long for garnishing

GREEN CURRY PASTE

2 tsp coriander (*dhania*) seeds, 1 tsp peppercorns (*saboot kali mirch*)

1 tsp cumin seeds (*jeera*) - roasted, 1 tsp fennel (*saunf*)

12 green chillies - chopped

¼ cup fresh basil leaves, ¼ cup chopped coriander leaves

½ onion - chopped, 1 tsp salt, ½ tsp grated nutmeg (*jaiphal*)

4 flakes garlic

2 thin slices of ginger, preferably galangal - chopped

1 stick lemon grass (use only the lower portion) - cut into pieces, discard the leaves

1   For the green curry paste, dry roast coriander, peppercorns, fennel and cumin seeds for 2 minutes on a tawa till fragrant but not brown. Put all other ingredients of the curry paste and the roasted seeds in a grinder and grind to a fine paste, using water.

2   Heat 3 tbsp oil in a pan. Add green curry paste. Fry for 2-3 minutes.

3   Add brinjals and chicken and again fry for 2-3 minutes.

4   Add ½ cup water, lower heat and simmer for 4-5 minutes or till chicken is nearly done.

5   Add salt, sugar, basil, fish sauce, lemon leaves, brinjal and coconut milk.

6   Boil. Cook on low heat till brinjal and chicken are well cooked.

7   Garnish with chillies (long thin slices), basil leaves and serve with boiled rice.

Note:

🪶 The Thais use the very small, marble sized green brinjals, whole in their dishes, without peeling. However the ordinary purple ones available easily, can also be used. Peel and cut into slices.

🪶 For lemon grass, Discard 1" from the bottom of the lemon grass. Peel a few outer leaves. Chop into ½" pieces uptil the stem. Discard upper grass like portion.

Crispy Chicken with Pineapple

Serves 3-4

250 gm chicken - cut into 1" pieces

2 slices of fresh or tinned pineapple - chopped, 1 fresh pineapple, optional

1 onion - cut into 8 pieces, 15-20 basil leaves - shredded

1 tbsp tomato ketchup, 1 tbsp stir fry sauce, 1 tsp honey

a pinch of salt & pepper, or to taste

MARINADE

1 egg, 2 tbsp finely chopped lemon grass, 1 tsp chopped garlic

2 dry red chillies, 1 tbsp white wine, ½ tsp pepper

½ tsp salt, 2 tbsp cornflour, 1" stick cinnamon (*dalchini*)

BATTER

¼ cup rice powder, ½ cup cornflour, 1 tbsp oil, ½ tsp soya sauce

1 tsp red chilli flakes, ½ tsp salt

1. Mixall ingredients of marinade in a flat bowl and add chicken to the prepared marinade. Keep aside for 5- 6 hours.

2. Mix all ingredients of batter in a bowl. Add enough cold water to get a thick coating batter.

3. Heat oil in a kadhai. Dip each piece of marinated chicken in batter so that a thick coating covers the chicken, covering on all the sides. Immediately deep fry till golden brown.

4. Heat 1 tbsp oil. Add onion and cook till soft. Add pineapple pieces and basil leaves and stir for 2 minutes.

5. Add honey, tomato ketchup, stir fry sauce, salt, pepper and mix well.

6. Add fried chicken and mix well. Serve hot in a hollowed warmed pineapple shell or in a bowl.

Chinese Kung Pao Chicken

Serves 4

450-500 gm boneless chicken breast - thinly sliced
2 spring onions (*hara pyaz*) - chopped, 8 dry red chillies - broken into half
1" piece of ginger - grated, 2 tsp crushed garlic
5 tbsp oil, 4 tbsp water mixed with ½ stock/soup cube, 2 tbsp cornflour
½ cup peanuts - dry roast on a griddle (*tawa*)

MARINADE
2 tbsp white wine, 2 tbsp oil, 2 tbsp soy sauce, 1 tsp salt, 2 tbsp cornflour

SAUCE
6 tbsp soy sauce, 4 tbsp white wine
6 tbsp rice vinegar or 4½ tbsp white vinegar + 1½ tbsp water
4 tbsp sugar, 4 tbsp oil

1. Chop the whites of spring onions into ½" pieces. Finely julienne the green portions. Keep aside.

2. Combine all the ingredients of the marinade in a bowl. Mix.

3. Add the chicken and mix to coat the pieces. Leave to marinate in the refrigerator for 20 to 30 minutes.

4. In another bowl, mix together all the ingredients for the sauce. Keep aside.

5. Heat oil in a wok or *kadhai* over high heat. Add the chillies, ginger, garlic and white part of the spring onions. Stir-fry for 30 to 40 seconds, or until the chillies turn dark.

6. Add the marinated chicken and stir-fry for 2-3 minutes, until chicken is cooked.

7. Pour in the prepared sauce. Bring to a boil. Add the peanuts.

8. Mix together the chicken stock and cornflour in a bowl. Add cornflour paste to the chicken. Continue to cook until the sauce is thick and glossy, and the chicken is soft.

9. Add spring onion greens. Remove. Serve immediately.

Stir-fried Chicken n Bok choy

Serves 4

MARINATE TOGETHER
2 chicken breasts - sliced
1 tbsp garlic paste, 1 tsp soya sauce , 1 tsp lemon juice, 1 tbsp oil
½ tsp each of salt and red chilli flakes

OTHER INGREDIENTS
2 bunches of bok choy - each leaf cut into 2 pieces (stem and leaf)
4-6 babycorns, 4-6 french beans, 1-2 carrots
1 red & yellow capsicum - cut into 1" squares
4-6 flakes garlic - slivered
4 tbsp oil, 1 tsp sesame oil
2 tsp sesame seeds, 4 tbsp stir fry sauce
1 tsp salt and ½ tsp pepper or to taste

FOR BLANCHING THE VEG'S
1 tsp salt, 1 tsp sugar, 1 tbsp lemon juice

1. Marinate chicken with 1 tbsp garlic paste, soya sauce, lemon juice, red chilli flakes, salt and 2 tbsp oil for 2-3 hours or more. Keep aside.

2. Boil 4-5 cups of water with 1 tsp salt, 1 tsp sugar and 1 tbsp lemon juice. Drop pok choy in boiling water. Remove after 30 seconds. Put carrot, babycorns and french beans in boiling water. As soon as the boil returns, keep boiling for 1 minute more. Remove from fire and strain the vegetables. Allow them to come to room temperature and dry.

3. Once the blanched vegetables have cooled down to room temperature, get ready for stir frying that is always done, just before serving.

4. Heat 1 tbsp oil in the wok. Add chicken and stir fry for 2 minutes till it changes colour. Check for doneness and remove from fire. Keep aside.

5. In the same wok, add 3 tbsp oil. Reduce heat, add the garlic and stir for ½ a minute and add the sesame seeds. Let them just change colour slightly and stir in the blanched vegetables.

6. Lastly the red and yellow capsicums. Stir fry on high flame for a minute.

7. Add the stir fried sliced chicken. Mix.

8. Add stir fry sauce and stir fry again for a minute. Transfer to a serving platter. Top with some sesame seeds. Drizzle some sauce on the sides if you like.

Thai Red Curry

Serves 4-6

RED CURRY PASTE

4 dry, kashmiri red chillies - deseeded & soaked in ½ cup warm water
for 10 minutes
½ tsp degi mirch powder
½ onion - chopped, 2 tbsp oil, 1 tsp salt, 1 tbsp lemon juice
8-10 flakes garlic - peeled(1 tbsp), ½" piece ginger - chopped(1 tsp)
1 stalk lemon grass, see note
1½ tsp coriander (*dhania*) seeds - roast, ½ tsp cumin (*jeera*) - roast
6 peppercorns (*saboot kali mirch*) - roast

OTHER INGREDIENTS

1 chicken breast - cut into ¾" cubes, 4-5 baby corns - slit lengthwise
5-6 florets broccoli/cauliflower - cut into small florets
1 cup thickly sliced mushrooms
2 cups ready made coconut milk, 1 cup water
½ tsp soya sauce, 2 tsp brown sugar, salt to taste
15 basil leaves, 5-6 lemon leaves whole, 2 tbsp oil

1. For the paste, roast coriander seeds, cumin seeds and peppercorns. Grind to a fine powder. Add the remaining ingredients of the paste to the grinder. Grind all the ingredients of the red curry paste along with the water in which the chillies were soaked, to a very fine paste.

2. Marinate chicken in the curry paste and refrigerate for a few hours.

3. Heat the oil in a large pan, add the chicken in red curry paste and fry for 2-3 minutes on medium heat till it changes colour.

4. Add vegetables and cook for 2-3 minutes.

5. Add the coconut milk, soya sauce and lemon leaves. Add water if you like a thin curry. Boil.

6. Add salt and sugar to taste. Add basil leaves. Simmer on low heat for 5-7 minutes till the chicken and vegetables are tender. Serve hot with steamed rice or noodles.

Chicken in Black Bean Sauce

Serves 4

250 gm boneless chicken (2 small thin breasts)

½ tsp salt, ½ tsp pepper, 1 tsp soya sauce, ½ tsp garlic paste

1 egg, 2 tbsp cornflour, 2 tbsp flour (*maida*)

SAUCE

1 tbsp oil

1 tbsp ginger-garlic - minced or very finely chopped

5 tbsp black bean sauce, ready-made

2 babycorns - sliced diagonally

a few juliennes of red bell-pepper

a few juliennes of yellow bell-pepper

a few juliennes of green capsicum

½ onion - cut into 4 pieces and separated

250 ml stock (1¼ cups) or 1¼ cup water mixed with 1 stock/soup cube

¼ tsp salt, or to taste, a pinch of ajinomoto

½ tsp sugar or to taste

½ tsp soya sauce, 1 tsp tomato ketchup, optional

4 tbsp cornflour dissolved in ½ cup water

1. Wash and pat dry chicken. Freeze chicken breast for 30 minutes. Cut cold chicken into thin strips with a sharp knife.

2. Mix cornflour and flour in a bowl. Add egg and mix very well to break all the lumps. Add soya sauce, salt, pepper and garlic. Add chicken to this mixture and keep aside for 20 minutes.

3. Heat oil for deep frying in a kadhai. Reduce heat. Add chicken strips. Deep fry for 1½ minutes till done. Do not over fry. Fry the chicken in 3-4 batches. Do not fry longer as it will turn the chicken hard. Keep aside.

4. For the sauce, heat oil and remove from fire. Add ginger-garlic. Do not let the ginger-garlic change colour to brown.

5. Add the black bean sauce and the vegetables. Stir for half a minute.

6. Add the stock, salt, ajinomoto, sugar and soya sauce. Boil.

7. Add the cornflour paste and mix well. Bring to a boil.

8. Add chicken. Simmer for 3-4 minutes till sauce turns thick. Add ketchup, if required. Serve it with rice or noodles.

Rice, Bread and Noodles

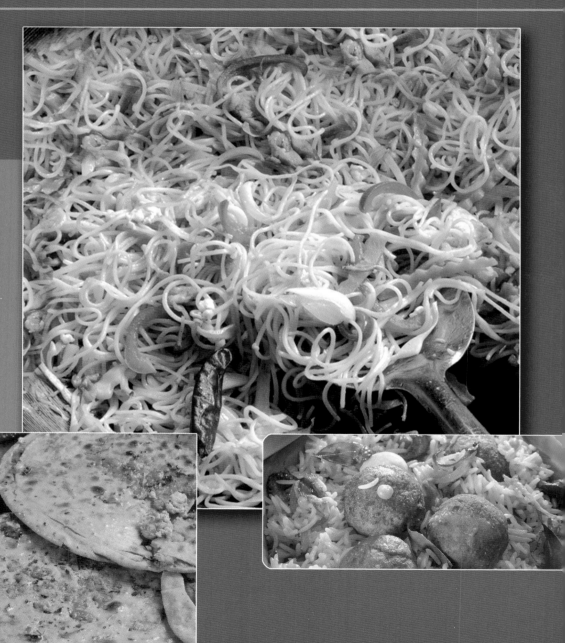

Chicken Fried Rice

Serves 4

1 cup uncooked rice (3 cups cooked rice)

3 tbsp oil

1 tbsp finely chopped garlic, 1 onion - finely chopped

2 green chillies - chopped, ½ tsp aji-no-moto, ½ cup chopped cabbage

1 capsicum - finely chopped

1 small boneless chicken breast (125 gm)

2 tsp salt, ½ tsp pepper powder, 2 tsp soya sauce

1. Wash rice. Strain and leave in the strainer for 10 minutes. Boil 5-6 cups water with 1 tsp salt and 1 tsp oil. Add rice and boil for about 7-8 minutes till almost done but firm to bite.

2. When done, strain, spread on a tray. Cool under a fan. Rice should remain separate.

3. Boil 2 cups water with ½ tsp salt. Add chicken and cook for about 5 minutes till soft and no longer pink from inside. Remove chicken and shred thinly into strips.

4. Heat oil in a wok. Add garlic & stir. Add onions & fry onion till very light brown.

5. Add green chillies and aji-no-moto.

6. Add cabbage and capsicum and stir fry for 1-2 minutes.

7. Add boiled shredded chicken. Saute for a minute. Add salt and pepper.

8. Add soya sauce. Mix well.

9. Add rice. Mix well. Stir fry for 3-4 minutes. Mix & remove from fire. Serve hot.

Biryani Masala Murg

Serves 4

2 cups basmati rice - soaked for 30 minutes in water

500 gms chicken, with or without bones - cut into 6 small pieces

4 tsp salt, 1 tsp turmeric powder (*haldi*)

5 cups ready-made coconut milk OR 12 tbsp coconut powder (2 packets of maggi coconut powder) mixed with 3 cups water and 2 cups milk

3½ tbsp lemon juice, 7 tbsp oil

PASTE (makes ½ cup approx.)

10 dried, red chillies , 2 onions - chopped

12-14 flakes of garlic, 4 tsp chopped ginger

2 tbsp cumin seeds (*jeera*), 2 tsp fennel (*saunf*)

2" stick cinnamon (*dalchini*)

seeds of 4 brown cardamom (*moti illaichi*)

¼ tsp grated nutmeg (*jaiphal*)

4 tbsp coriander (*dhania*) seeds, 4 cloves (*laung*)

8 black peppercorns (*saboot kali mirch*)

1. For the paste, roast all ingredients of the paste on a tawa/kadhai/wok for 5 minutes or till fragrant.

2. Grind to a fine paste. Use little water if needed.

3. Heat 7 tbsp oil in a deep pan with a well fitted lid. Add the chicken and bhuno for 7-8 minutes on medium flame till chicken gets golden brown from various sides.

4. Add prepared paste. Fry for about 3 minutes or till it leaves oil.

5. Reduce heat, add ½ cup of prepared coconut milk. Cook till nearly dry for about 2-3 minutes.

6. Add salt, turmeric, remaining coconut milk & the soaked rice. Mix well gently.

7. Give one boil. Reduce heat and cook covered on very low heat for 10-12 minutes or till all the water has dried and the rice is cooked. Shut of the flame.

8. Sprinkle lemon juice, mix gently with a fork.

9. Remove from fire and transfer to a serving plate. Separate the grains with a fork. Serve garnished with lemon wedges and tomato slices.

Tandoori Parantha

Serves 6

250 gm minced chicken (*keema*)
1 onion - chopped finely
2 tsp finely chopped ginger
1 tsp salt, 1 tsp coriander (*dhania*) powder, ½ tsp red chilli powder
½ tsp garam masala
2 green chillies - chopped
1 tbsp finely chopped fresh coriander
1 tbsp dry fenugreek leaves (*kasoori methi*)

DOUGH
2 cups wheat flour (*atta*), ½ tsp salt, 1 tbsp ghee

1   To prepare the dough, sift flour and salt. Rub in 1 tbsp ghee. Add enough water to make a dough. Keep aside for 30 minutes.

2   To prepare the filling, heat 2 tbsp of oil and stir fry the chopped onions until rich brown.

3   Add mince and ginger and mix well. Reduce heat. Add salt, coriander powder, red chilli powder and garam masala. Fry for 1-2 minutes. Cook covered on low heat for about 5 minutes, till the mince is cooked.

4   Add green chillies and 1 tbsp finely chopped coriander. If there is any water, uncover and dry the mince on fire. Keep the stuffing aside.

5   Divide the dough into 6 equal parts. Shape into round balls.

6   Flatten each ball, roll out each into a round of 5" diameter.

7   Spread 1 tsp full of ghee. Then spread 1-2 tbsp of filling all over.

8   Make a slit, starting from the centre till any one end.

9   Start rolling from the slit, to form an even cone.

10   Keeping the cone upright, press slightly.

11   Roll out, applying pressure only at the centre. Do not roll or press too much on the sides, otherwise the layers of parantha do not separate after cooking.

12   Sprinkle some dry fenugreek leaves and press with a rolling pin (*belan*).

13   Apply water on the back side of the parantha and stick carefully in a heated tandoor or place in a preheated oven in a greased tray.

14   Remove after a few minutes. Spread some ghee, serve hot.

Chicken Haka Noodles

Serves 4

3 tbsp oil, 200 gm shredded chicken
1 tsp chilli powder, 4-5 flakes garlic - crushed
2-3 spring onions - shredded diagonally, 1 capsicum - shredded
1 medium sized carrot - shredded, 50 gm cabbage - shredded
3-4 tbsp bean sprouts, 2 tbsp shredded bamboo
1 tbsp shredded mushrooms
2 tbsp soya sauce, 2 tsp vinegar, 1 cup chicken stock
½ tsp ajinomoto (optional), ½ tsp each of salt, sugar & pepper
1-2 tbsp cornflour dissolved in ½ cup water

NOODLES
100 gm noodles, ½ tsp chilli powder
½ tsp salt, 2 dried red chillies, 2 tsp soya sauce, 3-4 tbsp oil

1. Shred vegetables. In a frying pan, heat 3 tbsp oil, reduce heat and add chilli powder. Add garlic. Add the chicken pieces. Fry for 1-2 minutes to a pale colour.

2. Add onion, bean sprouts, bamboo shoots, mushrooms, capsicum, carrot and then cabbage. Stir fry for 1-2 minutes. Reduce heat and add the stock and all the other ingredients, except cornflour paste.

3. Give one boil and add cornflour paste. Cook till the sauce turns thick. Remove from fire and keep aside.

4. To boil the noodles, boil 5-6 cups water with 1 tsp salt. Boil the noodles in salted water for 3-4 minutes. Drain the water. Put the noodles under running water. Rub a little oil over the noodles. Spread on a tray to cool.

5. In a frying pan heat oil, reduce heat, add broken chillies and then chilli powder. Mix in the boiled noodles. Add salt and soya sauce. Stir fry for 2 minutes.

6. To serve, put noodles on a platter. Pour warm vegetables and chicken over it.

Chicken Kofta Pulao

Serves 6-8

CHICKEN KOFTAS (BOIL TOGETHER)
400 gms chicken mince (*keema*)
2" piece cinnamon (*dalchini*), 4-5 cloves (*laung*)
1 tbsp black cumin (*shah jeera*) seeds, 2-3 green cardamom (*chhoti elaichi*)
seeds of 2-3 black cardamom (*moti elaichi*),
1 cup grated fresh coconut, 6-8 flakes of garlic, 1" piece ginger
1½ tsp red chilli powder, 1 tsp coriander (*dhania*) powder
2 tsp salt, 1 tbsp whole wheat flour

TO COAT BALLS
8 tbsp plain flour (*maida*)

RICE
2½ cups basmati rice - soaked in water for 30 minutes
½ cup split bengal gram (*chana dal*) - soaked in water for 1 hour
½ cup curry leaves - washed and dried on a kitchen towel
3 tbsp cashewnuts (*kaju*), 3 tbsp raisins (*kishmish*)
4 onions - sliced and deep fried till golden, 2 green chillies - chopped
4 cloves (*laung*), 4 black cardamoms (*moti elaichi*)
2 bay leaves (*tej patta*), ½ tsp red chilli powder, 1 tsp garam masala

BOIL TOGETHER IN 4½ CUPS OF WATER AND KEEP ASIDE
2 stock cubes (maggi) - crushed, 2 tsp salt, 1-2 drops of orange colour

1. Wash channa dal and soak in water for an hour.

2. Wash rice and soak in water for 30 minutes.

3. Heat 1 cup oil for frying in a kadhai. Add dry curry leaves, fry till crisp. Add cashewnuts and fry till golden. Add raisins and fry till it swells. Remove from oil.

4. In the same oil add sliced onions and fry to a golden brown colour. Remove onions from oil. Take half of the fried onions and keep separately.

5. Put together in a deep pan - 4½ cups of water, stock cube, salt and orange colour. Give one boil and keep aside.

6. Boil chicken mince with all the ingredients written under chicken koftas in a pressure cooker. Give 3-4 whistles and cook on low heat for 2 minutes. Remove from fire. Let the pressure drop by itself. If any water is left, then dry on fire. Let it cool down.

7   Churn the boiled mince in a mixer-grinder, with half of the fried onions to get a very fine mince.

8   Shape mince into round balls. Make 20 small balls. Coat with dry maida.

9   Deep fry 2-3 balls at a time in medium hot oil till golden. Keep aside.

10 Drain rice. Drain channa dal. Keep aside.

11 To make rice, heat 6 tbsp oil in a heavy bottom deep pan (*patila*), add whole spices, bay leaves, chopped green chillies and channa dal to the pan and fry for 2-3 minutes till fragrant.

12 Add garam masala and red chilli powder. Mix.

13 Drain rice, add to pan and continue frying for 8-9 minutes, stirring gently.

14 Add prepared stock cube water. Bring to a boil.

15 Cover pan with a tight fitting lid and cook over low heat till rice is tender.

16 Place half of the rice in a micro proof or oven proof serving dish. Place half the meatballs over the rice. Sprinkle half of the onions and cashewnuts and raisins. Repeat the layer of rice, then balls, then onions and cashewnuts layer.

17 Cover the dish and keep aside till serving time.

18 At serving time, heat the dish in a microwave and serve hot. In absence of a microwave, keep a tawa on the flame and put the serving dish over it. Cook on very low heat for 5-7 minutes.

19 Serve hot with raita.

Hyderabadi Dumpukht Biryani

Serves 8

1 kg mutton - cut into small pieces

3 cups basmati rice - boil with ½ tsp turmeric added to the water

4 onions - ground to a paste in the mixer

2 tsp ginger paste

2" piece of raw green papaya - grate with the peel and grind to a paste with just a little water (use only 1 tsp green papaya paste for the recipe)

a few threads of saffron (*kesar*)

2 cups yogurt, ½ cup *ghee* or oil

2 bay leaves (*tej patta*), 1 black cardamom (*moti elaichi*)

1" stick cinnamon (*dalchini*)

8-10 peppercorns (*saboot kali mirch*), 8 green cardamoms (*chhoti elaichi*)

1½ tsp red chilli powder

½ tsp turmeric (*haldi*) powder, 2 tsp coriander (*dhania*) powder

½ cup milk, salt to taste

GRIND SPICES TOGETHER

1 tsp peppercorns (*saboot kali mirch*)

½ tsp cumin seeds (*jeera*)

6 cloves (*laung*), seeds of 2 black cardamoms (*moti elaichi*)

1   Wash mutton. Pat dry on a kitchen towel to drain out all water. Add 1½ tsp salt, a little saffron, onion paste, ginger paste and just 1 tsp papaya paste to the mutton. Rub the mixture well into the meat. Add the yogurt and the freshly ground spices. Set aside for at least 4-5 hours or overnight in the fridge.

2   Take a heavy-bottomed pan and heat oil or ghee in it. Add bay leaves, black cardamom, 1" stick cinnamon, peppercorns and green cardamoms. Wait for a minute for the spices to turn fragrant. Add the marinated mutton along with the marinade and stir continuously on high heat for 3-4 minutes. Add red chilli powder, turmeric, and coriander powder. Mix well. Cover and cook on low medium heat for about 20 minutes, stirring occasionally till mutton is almost cooked. Check salt and masalas and adjust to taste.

3   Take a handi or an oven-proof dish. Grease with oil. Put 1/3 of rice. Top with half the mutton. Again put half of the remaining rice and cover with the left over mutton. Top with rice. Sprinkle the milk on the rice. Cover the pan with a tight fitting lid or aluminium foil. Seal it with dough. Place the handi on a tawa on high heat for 5-7 minutes and then reduce heat and keep for 20-25 minutes so that the meat gets tender and the rice is done.

Murg Pulao

Serves 2

1 cup basmati rice - washed & soaked in 2 cups water for 30 minutes
250 gm chicken - cut into pieces
1 tsp salt, 2 tbsp oil

PASTE
3 dried, red chillies - deseeded, 2 onions - chopped,1 tbsp oil
½ tsp salt, ¼ tsp turmeric (*haldi*) powder, 12-14 flakes garlic - chopped
2 tsp chopped ginger , 1 tbsp cumin seeds (*jeera*), 2 tsp fennel (*saunf*)
1" stick cinnamon (*dalchini*), seeds of 2 black cardamoms (*moti elaichi*)
3 clover (*laung*), 8 peppercorns (*saboot kali mirch*)

1   Soak rice in 2 cups water for 30 minutes.

2   For the paste grind all ingredients together, using some water.

3   Mix chicken and the prepared paste. Marinate for 2-3 hours.

4   Heat oil. Add the chicken with the marinade and stir fry for 3-4 minutes till it changes colour.

5   Add rice along with the water. Add 1 tsp salt. Mix. Cover and cook on low heat for 13 minutes.

6   Separate the grains with a fork. Serve hot.

INTERNATIONAL CONVERSION GUIDE

These are not exact equivalents; they've been rounded-off to make measuring easier.

WEIGHTS & MEASURES

METRIC	IMPERIAL
15 g	½ oz
30 g	1 oz
60 g	2 oz
90 g	3 oz
125 g	4 oz (¼ lb)
155 g	5 oz
185 g	6 oz
220 g	7 oz
250 g	8 oz (½ lb)
280 g	9 oz
315 g	10 oz
345 g	11 oz
375 g	12 oz (¾ lb)
410 g	13 oz
440 g	14 oz
470 g	15 oz
500 g	16 oz (1 lb)
750 g	24 oz (1½ lb)
1 kg	30 oz (2 lb)

LIQUID MEASURES

METRIC	IMPERIAL
30 ml	1 fluid oz
60 ml	2 fluid oz
100 ml	3 fluid oz
125 ml	4 fluid oz
150 ml	5 fluid oz (¼ pint/1 gill)
190 ml	6 fluid oz
250 ml	8 fluid oz
300 ml	10 fluid oz (½ pint)
500 ml	16 fluid oz
600 ml	20 fluid oz (1 pint)
1000 ml	1¾ pints

CUPS & SPOON MEASURES

METRIC	IMPERIAL
1 ml	¼ tsp
2 ml	½ tsp
5 ml	1 tsp
15 ml	1 tbsp
60 ml	¼ cup
125 ml	½ cup
250 ml	1 cup

HELPFUL MEASURES

METRIC	IMPERIAL
3 mm	1/8 in
6 mm	¼ in
1 cm	½ in
2 cm	¾ in
2.5 cm	1 in
5 cm	2 in
6 cm	2½ in
8 cm	3 in
10 cm	4 in
13 cm	5 in
15 cm	6 in
18 cm	7 in
20 cm	8 in
23 cm	9 in
25 cm	10 in
28 cm	11 in
30 cm	12 in (1ft)

HOW TO MEASURE

When using the graduated metric measuring cups, it is important to shake the dry ingredients loosely into the required cup. Do not tap the cup on the table, or pack the ingredients into the cup unless otherwise directed. Level top of cup with a knife. When using graduated metric measuring spoons, level top of spoon with a knife. When measuring liquids in the jug, place jug on a flat surface, check for accuracy at eye level.

OVEN TEMPERATURE

These oven temperatures are only a guide. Always check the manufacturer's manual.

	°C (Celsius)	°F (Fahrenheit)	Gas Mark
Very low	120	250	1
Low	150	300	2
Moderately low	160	325	3
Moderate	180	350	4
Moderately high	190	375	5
High	200	400	6
Very high	230	450	7

HERBS & SPICES

ENGLISH NAME	HINDI NAME
1 Asafoetida	1 Hing
2 Bay Leaves	2 Tej Patta
3 Cardamom	3 Elaichi, Chhoti Elaichi
4 Cardamom, Black	4 Moti Elaichi
5 Carom Seeds	5 Ajwain
6 Chillies, Green	6 Hari Mirch
7 Chillies, Dry Red	7 Sukhi Saboot Lal Mirch
8 Chilli Powder, Red	8 Lal Mirch Powder
9 Cinnamon	9 Dalchini
10 Cloves	10 Laung
11 Coriander Seeds	11 Saboot Dhania
12 Coriander Seeds, ground	12 Dhania Powder
13 Coriander Leaves	13 Hara Dhania
14 Cumin Seeds	14 Jeera
15 Cumin Seeds, black	15 Shah Jeera
16 Curry Leaves	16 Kari Patta
17 Fennel Seeds	17 Saunf
18 Fenugreek Seeds	18 Methi Dana
19 Fenugreek Leaves, Dried	19 Kasuri Methi
20 Garam Masala Powder	20 Garam Masala
21 Garlic	21 Lahsun
22 Ginger	22 Adrak
23 Mace	23 Javitri
24 Mango Powder, Dried	24 Amchur
25 Melon Seeds	25 Magaz
26 Mint Leaves	26 Pudina
27 Mustard Seeds	27 Rai, Sarson
28 Nigella, Onion Seeds	28 Kalaunji
29 Nutmeg	29 Jaiphal
30 Peppercorns	30 Saboot Kali Mirch
31 Pomegranate Seeds, Dried	31 Anardana
32 Sesame Seeds	32 Til
33 Saffron	33 Kesar
34 Turmeric Powder	34 Haldi

BEST SELLING COOKBOOKS BY

101 Recipes for Children

Permanen Weight Loss Cookbook

Cookbook for Controlling DIABETES

101 Diet Recipes

Step by Step Chocolate Cookbook

Cake & Cake Decorations

Zero Oil Cooking

Cooking for Growing Children

101 Vegetarian Recipes

Indian Favourites

101 International Recipes

101 Microwave Recipes

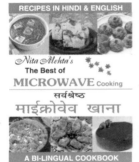

The Best of Microwave Cooking

Lebanese cooking for the Indian kitchen

Mother & Child Cookbook

Flavours of Indian Cooking